WELCOME TO THE FAMILY HISTORY WORKBOOK FOR *BEGINNERS*

This is so exciting – welcome to the world of family history. I'm guessing that you're super-keen to start tracing your family story and grow a really smashing family tree. Perhaps you have a family mystery you'd like to solve, and maybe you're even thinking about taking a DNA test. Well, you've come to the right place. We can help you.

Within the pages of the *Family History Workbook for Beginners* you will discover step-by-step guides, tips to help you search smarter, advice on the key records and websites to use to find your ancestors, plus hacks to help you save time, keep tip-top organised and make the most of absolutely every moment you have doing your family history.

Wishing you all the best with your future discoveries, and if ever you have a query, just drop us a line. Enjoy your genealogy!

Helen

Helen Tovey
Editor *Family Tree*
helen.t@family-tree.co.uk

The Family History Workbook for Beginners is published by Warners Group Publications plc, 5th Floor, 31-32 Park Row, Leeds LS1 5JD, UK and printed by Warners (Midlands) plc, The Maltings, West Street, Bourne, Lincolnshire PE10 9PH, UK. © 2023 Family Tree/Warners Group Publications plc

The publishers of the Family History Workbook for Beginners welcome corrections or additions, which will be considered for future editions.

The Family History Workbook for Beginners was created by the Family Tree team: Helen Tovey, Rachel Bellerby, Rajneet Gill and Jackie Grainger.

Editorial contact: editorial@family-tree.co.uk
Multimedia Advertising Account Manager: mark.dean@warnersgroup.co.uk
Publisher: Matthew Hill
Editor: Helen Tovey
Deputy Editor: Rachel Bellerby
Multimedia Advertising
Account Manager: Mark Dean
Marketing Manager: Hope Varnes
Senior Designer: Nathan Ward
Designer: Rajneet Gill, Jackie Grainger

Images: Cover tree image by Natalia/AdobeStock, girl with laptop by N_studio/AdobeStock; P14-15 Tree vector by green2/AdobeStock; P16-17 chart image by New Africa/AdobeStock; P20-23 hand and laptop by John Schnobrich/Unsplash; P24-27 outdoor office vector by ribkhan/AdobeStock; P28-31 books by L.Darin/AdobeStock, people in black, coral and yellow by rikkyal/AdobeStock man on book by Rogatnev/AdobeStock; P32-35, people in purple and yellow by rikkyal/AdobeStock; P40-p41 people and science vector by artinspiring/AdobeStock; P42-45 people on campus by Mariusz S/peopleimages.com/AdobeStock, young woman by Good Faces/Unsplash, education vector by creativeteam/AdobeStock; P46-49 Top archive websites, purple screen vector by Olesia_g/AdobeStock; P50-51 files & people vector by Bro Vector/AdobeStock; P56-59 by Visual Generation/AdobeStock, archive image by trattieritratti/AdobeStock, to-do by Ico Maker/AdobeStock; P60-62 colourful books by Garmin B/AdobeStock; P64-65 yellow and green vector by makyzz/AdobeStock; P68-71 book and people and book and trees by Marina Zlochin/AdobeStock; P80-86 clipboard and people and desk and people by nakigitsune-sama/AdobeStock; P90-93 woman and microscope/AdobeStock by Nataliya Kalabina/AdobeStock, people and helix by tasty_cat/AdobeStock; P98-99 woman with laptop by Prostock-studio/AdobeStock, hands and laptop by vejaa/AdobeStock.

CONTENTS

The Family History Workbook for Beginners

HOW TO USE YOUR FAMILY HISTORY WORKBOOK FOR BEGINNERS

What's inside the *Workbook*?

The *Family History Workbook for Beginners* is a very practical guide to doing family history.

- Within the pages of your *Workbook* you'll find advice on how to search for your ancestors.
- There are check-lists for you to keep a note of your progress.
- The step-by-step guides will help you try things out, such as building an online family tree or exploring an essential family history website.

Who is the *Workbook* aimed at?

The advice within the pages of the *Family History Workbook for Beginners* is suitable for anyone wishing to start doing their family history.

The focus of the websites mentioned and the key record types mentioned are on ancestors from England, Wales, Scotland and Ireland.

That said, there is much advice that is useful for family history enthusiasts wherever your ancestors lived in the world:

- the advice on searching smarter;
- building accurate online family trees;
- learning how to explore archives and websites;
- tips on keeping organised and how to keep great family history notes;
- plus the coverage of DNA …

all these topics and more are relevant for family history fans the world over.

Some of the topics are popular topics published in previous issues of *Family Tree* and the *Family History Handbook*; many have been specifically created for the *Family History Workbook for Beginners*.

Don't miss out on your downloads!

You'll also find mentions of the *Family History Workbook for Beginners* hub page. From this hub page you'll be able to download family tree charts, research logs, check lists and video guides. Be sure to check it out:

https://www.family-tree.co.uk/information/fhwfb

Where to start?

The *Workbook* is designed to be your guide-by-your-side and covers many of the key questions and topics that people have when starting out on their family history. Each topic has been designed to work as a standalone read, providing you with the advice you need, there and then – so that you can dive in and start where you wish (you don't need to begin at the beginning!). Have fun!

How Ancestry™ can help you do YOUR FAMILY HISTORY

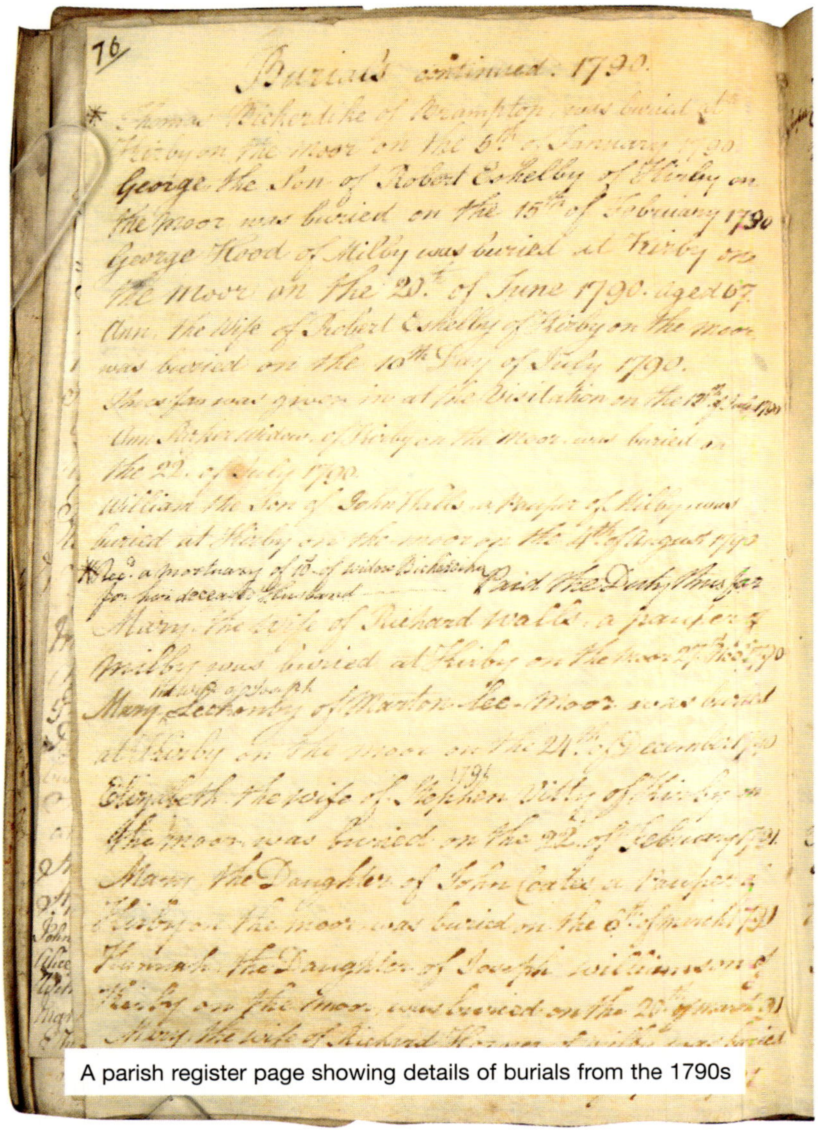

A parish register page showing details of burials from the 1790s

Are you looking to trace your family history and build an awesome online family tree? To explore historical records on the web, to find interesting clues about your ancestors? To check out your DNA and see what it can tell you about your origins? We can help with all this, and more. In fact Ancestry.co.uk exists to help you get to know your family story… better and better.

Join our dedicated online community of family history enthusiasts from around the globe, build your family tree online, and discover the records of history that include your ancestors: welcome to Ancestry.

How to get started

Everyone is welcome to build a family tree on Ancestry:

You just need to register for an account, and begin building your tree. You start with yourself, and gradually add the details of your parents and grandparents. You can grow your trees (yes – 'trees', you can have many online family trees with Ancestry, not just the one) as large as you wish.

Tip: Turn to page 36 of the Workbook to find out more about building your online tree with Ancestry.

Explore the historical records:

At some point when doing family history, everyone reaches the end of the road when it comes to what they *already* know. For instance, you've added all the names, dates and places that you know about the generations before you to your family tree.

Now what? It is at that point that you need to turn to the records of history to help you discover more.

Ancestry has a vast collection of historical records, spanning five centuries, and numerous countries from around the globe. The collections contain the key name-rich records used in family history; for the UK and Ireland, these would be the indexes of births, marriages and deaths, the parish registers of baptisms, marriages and burials, and the census records.

These records are just the start of your family story however. By exploring the military, immigration and emigration records, those for trade, schools, land, maps, finance and wills, you will be able to find out not just the 'book-end dates' of (births and deaths) for your ancestors, but will get a greater understanding of the lives they led, the work they did, the places they dwelt, the journeys they made and more - much more.

AncestryDNA has the largest database of autosomal DNA test-takers:

So far 22 million people from around the globe have tested with Ancestry and this number continues to grow.

Why is this so important? Because the larger the database, the more DNA matches you are likely to find – and those DNA matches are your kin! They are living people with whom you share direct ancestors.

Working out how you are related to each other is valuable for many reasons – it could help you solve a family history puzzle, identify ancestors, perhaps even aid you in tracing an unknown parent or grandparent. Your kin may have other family information, documents and photos that they are willing to share copies of with you. And lastly – working with your DNA for family history is truly rewarding.

Tip: Turn to page 94 of the Workbook to find out more about using your AncestryDNA test results.

The collections

On the following pages we are going to dive into a just a few of the 33,242 collections available on Ancestry. Over the past year at Ancestry has launched 45 new collections, encompassing 4.5 million images, and have updated a further 23 collections. To explore the full range visit **www.ancestry.com/search/collections/catalog**

PARISH RECORDS OF BAPTISMS, MARRIAGES & BURIALS

Using parish registers in family history

The parish registers of ancestors' baptisms, marriages and burials contain the key clues to your ancestors' names, dates and places. Often they record relationships too (for instance, a baptism will likely name the father). As such they are of huge importance in tracing your family tree back many centuries – back to the 1500s.

It was King Henry VIII's top civil servant, Thomas Cromwell, who passed a decree in 1538 requiring every parish in England and Wales to keep a register of the baptisms, marriages and burials that took place within it. The registers continued to be kept, with increasing detail and survival rates, and are still being added to, to this day.

The parish registers are particularly useful to help to trace your ancestors in Victorian times and the early 20th century, enriching the details you may find for these ancestors in the census, and civil registers of births, marriages and burials. In addition they allow you to take your research back into the 18th century and even further back in time.

Hardwicke & Rose: improvements to the parish registers

Lord Hardwicke's Marriage Act 1754 enacted that separate registers of marriage must be kept from 1755 onwards, and pre-printed forms came into use, although this did not happen immediately across all parishes. Politician George Rose similarly pressed for further improvements to the parish record-keeping and his 'An Act for the better regulating and preserving Parish and other Registers of Births, Baptisms, Marriages, and Burials, in England' led to the introduction of separate registers for baptisms and burials from 1813 onwards.

STEP-BY-STEP

Ancestry has hundreds of data collections within its 'UK Parish Baptism, Marriage and Burial Records' largely covering locations in England, Wales and Scotland too.

STEP 1

Go to **www.ancestry.co.uk/search/categories/epr/** to begin searching all the UK parish registers available on Ancestry.

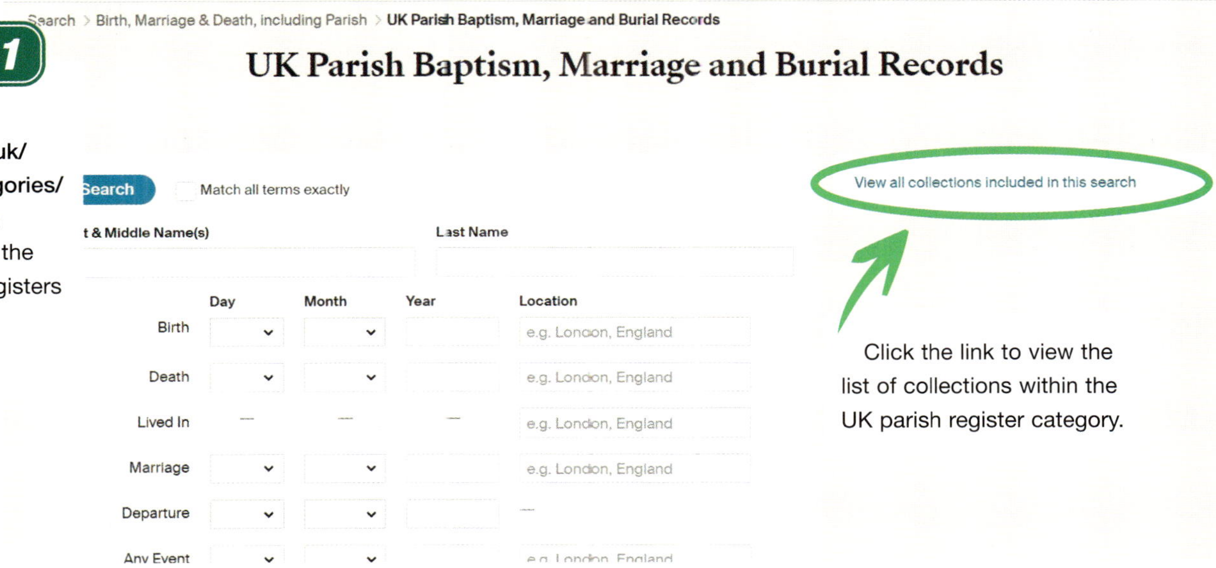

Click the link to view the list of collections within the UK parish register category.

STEP 2

By way of example, let's look at the collection of 'North Yorkshire, England, Church of England Baptisms, Marriages and Burials, 1558-1812' records.

This is the latest parish register collection to be added to Ancestry and includes more than 2.6 million records spanning 1558-1812.

STEP 3

Here are a list of search results. You can see some details, but to to view the full details of the search result and to click through to view any associated images of the original document you will need to upgrade.

If you haven't already, you can take a 14-day free trial. Membership costs from £10.99 a month after the free trial for a UK Essentials membership.

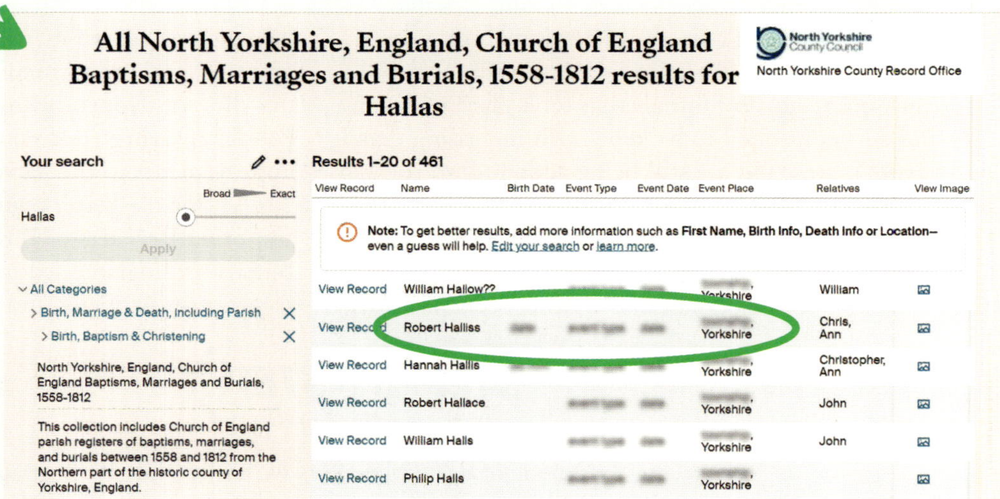

STEP 4

View Record	William Hallow??		Baptism	7 Dec 1710	Burnsall, Yorkshire	William	
View Record	Robert Halliss	11 Apr 1800	Baptism	10 May 1800	Wykeham, Yorkshire	Chris, Ann	
View Record	Hannah Hallis	15 Dec	Baptism	24 Dec 1797	Wykeham, Yorkshire	Christopher, Ann	
View Record	Robert Hallace		Baptism	14 Jun 1768	Hubberholme, Yorkshire	John	
View Record	William Halls		Burial	4 Aug 1790	Kirby on the Moor, Yorkshire	John	
View	[illegible]		[illegible]	9 Oct	Knaresborough: St John the		

Once you've upgraded, now you'll be able to view the full details of the search result, including the date and precise place.

For instance here we learn that Robert Halliss was born on 11 April 1800 and baptised on 10 May, and the event (the baptism) took place in Wykeham.

Source Citation
North Riding Record Office; Scarborough, North Riding of Yorkshire, England; *Parish Registers for North Yorkshire*; Reference: *PR/WYK 1/7*

STEP 5

Next click through to view the transcribed details clearly listed. These can be very useful when dealing with old records as the handwriting can be difficult to decipher.

You'll also see a preview of the digitised copy of the original record. It can be easy to take them for granted, but here we're looking at a record that is more than two centuries old.

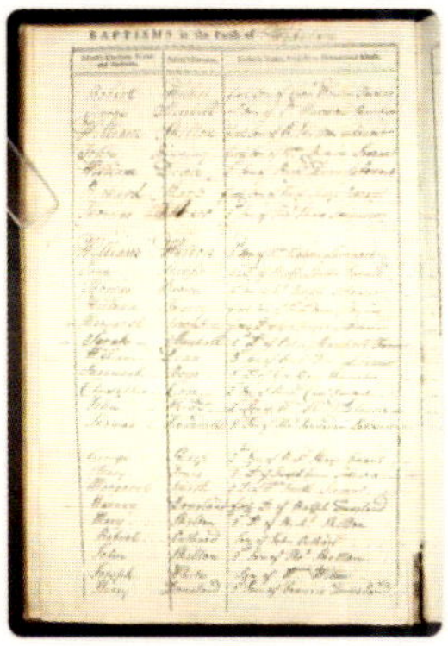

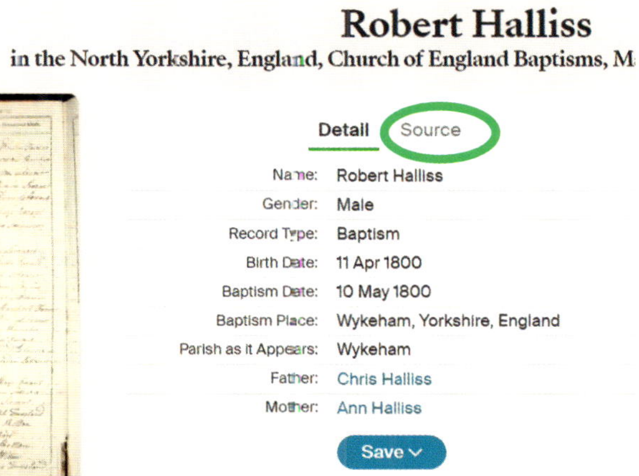

As well as gleaning the facts about your ancestor, note too that Ancestry also provide a 'source citation', for you to add to your research to prove where you found the details.

STEP 6

Be sure to study the original record!

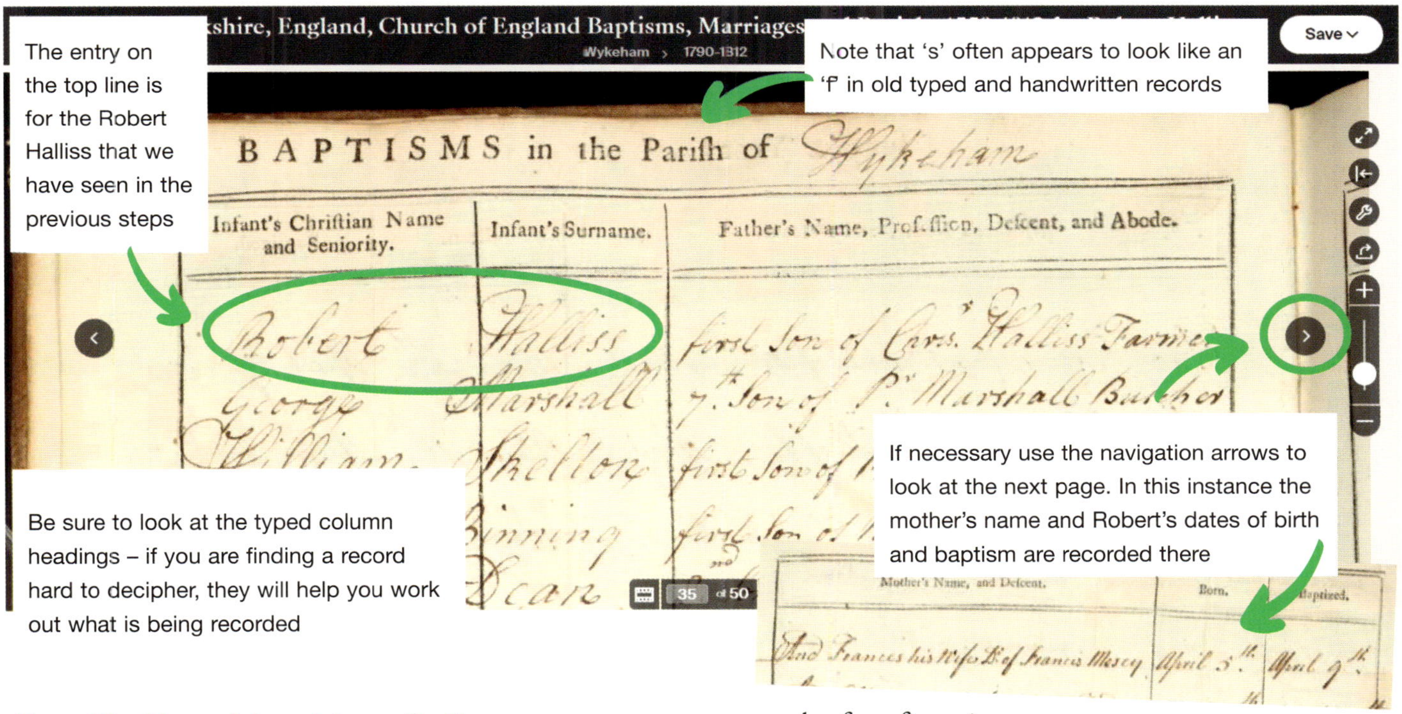

The entry on the top line is for the Robert Halliss that we have seen in the previous steps

Note that 's' often appears to look like an 'f' in old typed and handwritten records

Be sure to look at the typed column headings – if you are finding a record hard to decipher, they will help you work out what is being recorded

If necessary use the navigation arrows to look at the next page. In this instance the mother's name and Robert's dates of birth and baptism are recorded there

If you like the parish register collections, you may also like...

Within the data collections on Ancestry can be found many other types of records relating to baptisms, marriages and end of life.

They include, for instance:

- Non-conformist records of baptism, marriage and burial
- calendars of marriage licence allegations
- records of confirmations
- cemetery registers
- abstracts of wills and other probate records
- Bishop's Transcripts
- & annals and histories of selected parishes

Check out the newest collections on Ancestry using the Ancestry card catalog: www.ancestry.co.uk/search/collections/catalog

UK, WORLD WAR II WAR DIARIES, 1939-1946

Using World War II War Diaries in family history

Our ancestors' war years form a very significant chapter in our family history. You may have photographs of ancestors in uniform, may have seen their medals and perhaps heard stories of their experiences serving during the Second World War. How do you go about discovering more?

The Ancestry collection of 'UK World War II War Diaries, 1939-1946' includes more than 66,000 records and can help you find out more about the unit your ancestor served with. The diaries were produced for units of the British Army, the Indian Army, dominion forces under British command from Canada, New Zealand, South Africa and India, and allied and colonial troops under British command.

Diaries were kept by units at all levels, from battalions to entire military branches. The format of the diaries vary, but generally include regular entries that provide information about the activities of a unit. Some diaries offer more narrative detail than others. Notes about new instructions and troop movements, assessments of troop strength, and requests for reinforcements are common diary entry topics.

STEP-BY-STEP

STEP 1

Go to **www.ancestry.co.uk/search/collections/62376/** to begin searching the UK World War II diaries available on Ancestry.

Browse the links for details of dates and places.

The UK World War II diaries is a new release on Ancestry (late 2022). The diaries published so far cover important military events, such as the Second Battle of El Alamein (23 October – 11 November 1942).

STEP 2

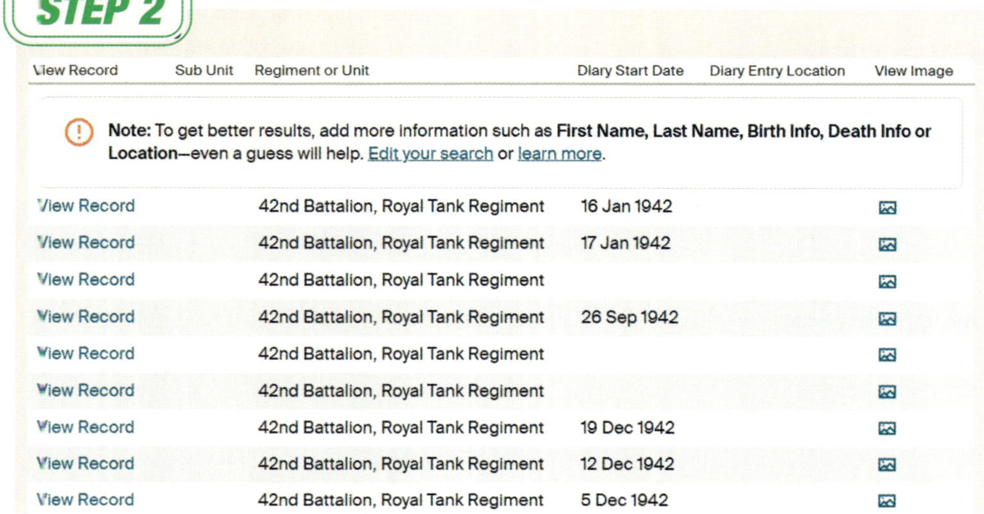

View Record	Sub Unit	Regiment or Unit	Diary Start Date	Diary Entry Location	View Image
Note: To get better results, add more information such as **First Name, Last Name, Birth Info, Death Info** or **Location**—even a guess will help. Edit your search or learn more.					
View Record		42nd Battalion, Royal Tank Regiment	16 Jan 1942		
View Record		42nd Battalion, Royal Tank Regiment	17 Jan 1942		
View Record		42nd Battalion, Royal Tank Regiment			
View Record		42nd Battalion, Royal Tank Regiment	26 Sep 1942		
View Record		42nd Battalion, Royal Tank Regiment			
View Record		42nd Battalion, Royal Tank Regiment			
View Record		42nd Battalion, Royal Tank Regiment	19 Dec 1942		
View Record		42nd Battalion, Royal Tank Regiment	12 Dec 1942		
View Record		42nd Battalion, Royal Tank Regiment	5 Dec 1942		

Search for your ancestors' unit name, for instance that of the regiment or squadron they served with.

STEP 3

From the search results, click through for greater index details and a preview of the digitised page.

(As with the parish registers, note the link to the 'source' information too)

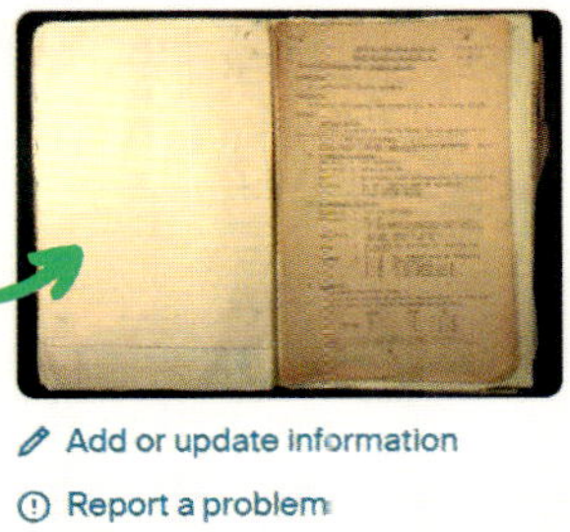

STEP 4

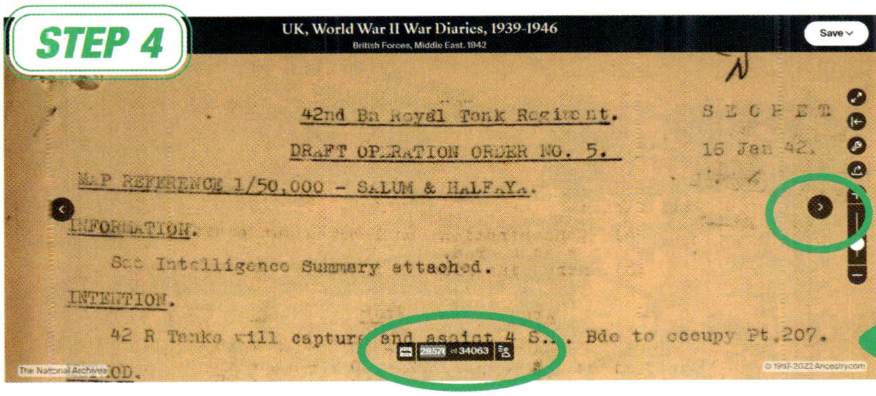

Use the arrows or page navigation tool at the bottom of the screen to work through the subsequent pages.

The page navigation tool is useful when exploring all sorts of collections on Ancestry.

Study the original page in detail.
Records in this collection may include the following information:

- Commanding officer's name and rank
- Regiment or unit
- Division
- Diary entry date
- Diary entry location

As always, be sure to explore the surrounding pages for further information

STEP 5

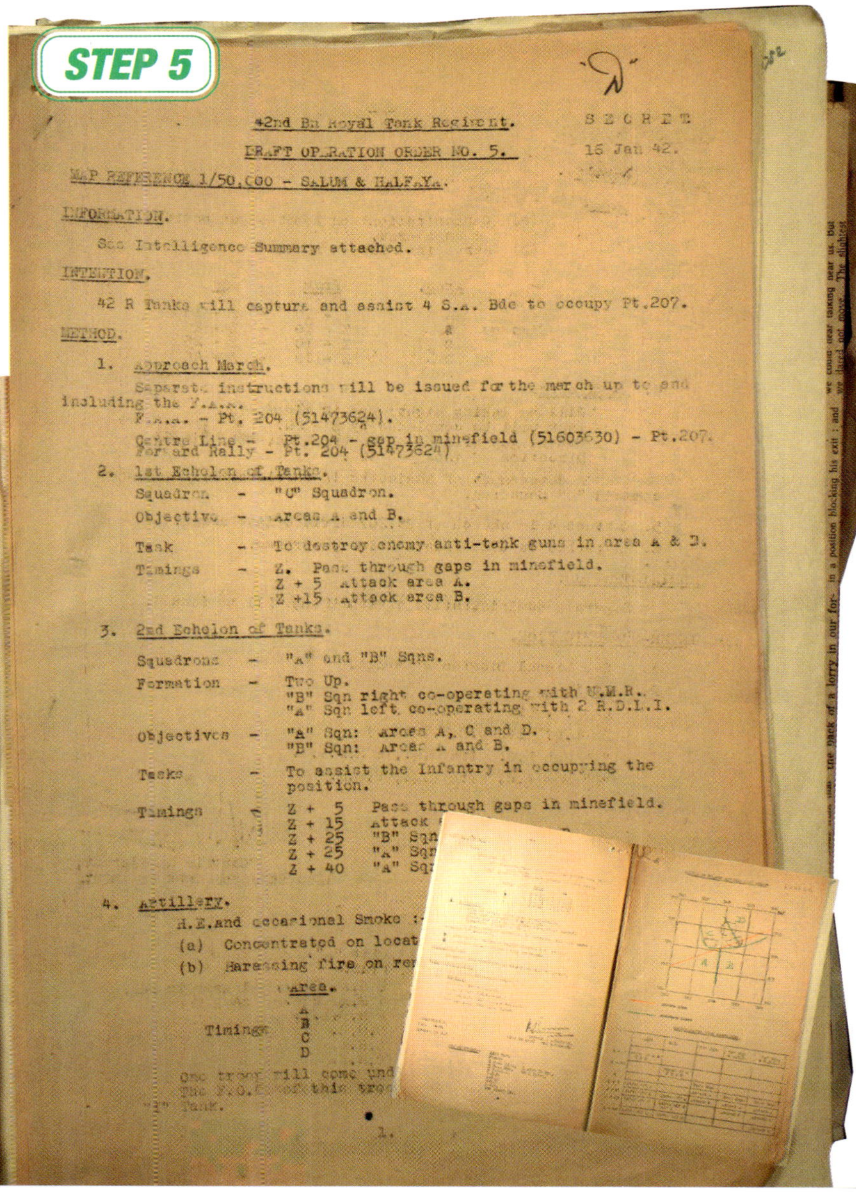

If you like these Second World War collections, you may also like...

Other records covering ancestors during the Second World War (and often a wider date-span) to search on Ancestry include:

- World War II Women's Land Army Index Cards, 1939-1948
- Scotland, National War Memorial Index, 1914-1945
- UK, Royal Air Force Operations Record Books, 1911-1963
- UK, Military Records of Baptisms, Confirmations, Marriages and Burials, 1813-1957
- UK, Royal Navy Officer Patrol Service Cards, 1904-1970
- UK, World War II Index to Allied Airmen Roll of Honour, 1939-1945
- Lancashire, England, World War II Home Guard Records, 1940-1945

Starting your family history for FREE

Follow these easy steps below, to get going without parting with a penny!

Family history is a really versatile hobby. Just by grabbing a notebook and phoning a relation, you can begin to gather clues about your family tree. Of course, not everyone has relations to call, but fortunately the internet is a treasure trove of family history records, too, which all of us can enjoy searching for clues.

3 easy steps to start your family history today!

❶ **Get a notebook and start jotting down what you know** about your family (your name, birthday and birth place; then do the same for your parents and then your grandparents). The notebook can be paper or digital (the main point is that you get into the habit of writing it all down. You won't regret this!).

- Write all the details down.
- Jot down any family memories anecdotes you know of.
- In addition, make a note of any questions about your family that you would like to find the answers to.

❷ **Start filling in a simple family tree,** using the clues you have added to your notebook.

Download printable family tree charts from the *Family History Workbook for Beginners*' resources web page: **www.family-tree.co.uk/information/fhwfb**

❸ **Sign up to start creating an online family tree.** You will need to register with whichever website you choose, but having done so you will be able to grow your tree online free of charge. The following websites are just some of those that provide free online tree-building tools:

- Ancestry.co.uk
- FamilySearch.org.uk
- Findmypast.co.uk
- MyHeritage.com
- TreeView.co.uk from TheGenealogist.co.uk

The websites we've just listed are linked to subscription services. This means that to view original records and limited-access databases you may have to subscribe (pay) to the relevant site. That said, FamilySearch is slightly different: it is a completely free site, it does work with partners, some of whom charge for access to their full records.

A golden rule

Before we go any further, here's a golden rule that you'll be so pleased you learned!

Start with what you DO know, and work BACKWARDS in time, carefully linking each piece of information.

A golden rule when starting family history is to begin with yourself, then note down what you know about your parents and grandparents, and work backwards in time. Ask your family members what they know too. They may know names and dates you don't, and may have stories and photos to share.

FREE genealogy websites to search

Many people want to trace their family tree for free and this can be a really good idea, particularly when you're just starting out.

Luckily there are some excellent websites and online resources to help. The sites listed below won't cost you a penny. Some have records for you to search for clues, some have an online tree building tool, and some have useful information, guides and web links.

FreeBMD: www.freebmd.org.uk

- This website provides a searchable index to birth, marriage and death records for England and Wales.

GRO: www.gro.gov.uk

- You can also search for ancestors' birth and death index entries at **www.gro.gov.uk/gro/content/certificates/login.asp** (this is also the site from which you order birth, marriage and death certificates for England and Wales, charges apply for the certificates).

My getting started check list

I've started keeping a family history notebook: YES ☐

I've started writing down memories & family anecdotes: YES ☐

I've downloaded the family tree charts from **family-tree.co.uk/information/fhwfb**: YES ☐

FreeCen: www.freecen.org.uk

• Sister site to FreeBMD, FreeCEN is aimed at providing 19th-century census record details free online. FreeCEN is part of the FreeUKGen project, along with FreeReg (the latter concentrating on parish registers, which are also very useful records for family history research).

FamilySearch: www.familysearch.org

• FamilySearch is the world's largest, free, genealogy site with billions of searchable historical records and research guidance via its Research Wiki, online courses and more.

UKBMD: www.ukbmd.org.uk

• With 2,792 links to sites useful for birth, marriage, death and census records for the UK, this is a website worth visiting. Some of the links provide material freely; for others, charges apply.

World Wide Web Directory

Cyndi's List is a labour of love by American Cyndi Howells. The list is an enormous, constantly updated, categorised index of more than three hundred thousand genealogical links worldwide – explore the topics, countries &, records.

Turn to page 54 of the *Workbook* to discover more about Cyndi's List

UK Web Directory

The UK and Ireland Genealogical Information Service by GENUKI is a virtual reference library of genealogical data, with links to all the county record offices in the UK, family history societies and much more.

MY ONLINE FAMILY TREE CHECK LIST

I've started exploring websites with a view to growing an online family tree:

Ancestry.co.uk: **YES** ☐

My thoughts: ....

....

....

....

FamilySearch.org.uk: **YES** ☐

My thoughts: ....

....

....

....

Findmypast.co.uk: **YES** ☐

My thoughts: ....

....

....

....

MyHeritage.com: **YES** ☐

My thoughts: ....

....

....

....

TreeView.co.uk: **YES** ☐

My thoughts: ....

....

....

MY FAMILY TREE CHART

2x great-grandfather
Name: ....
....
Date of birth: ....
Date of death: ....

2x great-grandmother
Name: ....
....
Date of birth: ....
Date of death: ....

2x great-grandfather
Name: ....
....
Date of birth: ....
Date of death: ....

2x great-grandmother
Name: ....
....
Date of birth: ....
Date of death: ....

2x great-grandfather
Name: ....
....
Date of birth: ....
Date of death: ....

2x great-grandmother
Name: ....
....
Date of birth: ....
Date of death: ....

2x great-grandfather
Name: ....
....
Date of birth: ....
Date of death: ....

2x great-grandmother
Name: ....
....
Date of birth: ....
Date of death: ....

Great-grandfather
Name: ....
....
Date of birth: ....
Date of death: ....
....

Great-grandmother
Name: ....
....
....
Date of birth: ....
Date of death: ....

Great-grandfather
Name: ....
....
....
Date of birth: ....
Date of death: ....

Great-grandmother
Name: ....
....
....
Date of birth: ....
Date of death: ....

Grandfather
Name: ....
....
....
Date of birth: ....
Date of death: ....

Grandmother
Name: ....
....
....
Date of birth: ....
Date of death: ....

Father
Name: ....
....
....
Date of birth: ....
Date of death: ....

1 Have a think about what you know

When starting your family history it's a good idea to have a think about what you already know. There will be gaps in your knowledge – don't worry if there are – we all have things we don't know, mysteries to solve, questions we're seeking the answers to.

Can your relations help?

It might be that you have family members who can help you. Older people's memories can hold valuable clues to the past, and your relations may have family papers, photos and mementoes with clues about people's names and birthdays, for instance, that you can glean for your family tree. If possible, be sure to ask your relations for help.

2 Fill in the family tree chart

Write in the details that you do know on the family tree chart above. This will give you a clear idea how much you know – and what you need to find out next.

Tip!
If you're unsure of any facts, use a pencil so you can easily amend the details when you find out more

2x great-grandfather
Name: ....
....
Date of birth: ....
Date of death: ....

2x great-grandmother
Name: ....
....
Date of birth: ....
Date of death: ....

2x great-grandfather
Name: ....
....
Date of birth: ....
Date of death: ....

2x great-grandmother
Name: ....
....
Date of birth: ....
Date of death: ....

2x great-grandfather
Name: ....
....
Date of birth: ....
Date of death: ....

2x great-grandmother
Name: ....
....
Date of birth: ....
Date of death: ....

2x great-grandfather
Name: ....
....
Date of birth: ....
Date of death: ....

2x great-grandmother
Name: ....
....
Date of birth: ....
Date of death: ....

Great-grandfather
Name: ....
....
....
Date of birth: ....
Date of death: ....

Great-grandmother
Name: ....
....
....
Date of birth: ....
Date of death: ....

Great-grandfather
Name: ....
....
....
Date of birth: ....
Date of death: ....

Great-grandmother
Name: ....
....
....
Date of birth: ....
Date of death: ....

Grandfather
Name: ....
....
....
Date of birth: ....
Date of death: ....

Grandmother
Name: ....
....
....
Date of birth: ....
Date of death: ....

Mother
Name: ....
....
....
Date of birth: ....
Date of death: ....

This is the family tree of
Name: ....
Date of birth: ....
Spouse: ....
Siblings: ....
....

3 Create several family trees

Remember, you can create as many family trees as you wish.

P.S. This chart is also available to download from your Beginners' Workbook Hub: www.family-tree.co.uk/information/bwbr. Create as many copies as you wish for your personal and family use

WHERE should I start my family history?

Here are a few simple tactics to help you work out where to start your family history. They will help you think about:

- what it is you wish to find out
- where to locate that information
- how to build an online family tree
- & will DNA help you?

In tracing your family history you will learn so many fascinating new things. These tactics below are to help you make the most of your research time and energy and have the maximum fun along the way.

Question 1: What do you wish to find out?

This is a great question to ask – 'What do you wish to find out?' as it will keep your thoughts organised: you are setting yourself a RESEARCH GOAL. You can break your goal down into bitesize chunks. For instance:

Q: 'What do you wish to find out?'

A: 'To trace my mother's family.'

This can be broken down into:

i. Finding my mother's birth certificate – and noting the names of the parents on the birth certificate – i.e. finding the names of your grandparents.

ii. Finding my mother's marriage certificate – and noting the occupation of her father and any addresses provided. Be sure to look at the names of the witnesses too (are they friends or relations?).

As you can see by the example above, a record such as a certificate can hold many clues that relate to numerous people. i.e. a marriage certificate doesn't just give clues about the bride and groom.

TIP! Get into the habit of looking carefully at every record you find. It's tempting to rush on to the next thing. However, by taking the time to explore all the details you will be helping yourself to discover more – there and then.

Question 2: Where will you find the records?

This depends where in the world your ancestors were. Each country organises its records differently: some have many national collections, whereas others are held at a more localised level. An excellent place to start finding out about the records available for your country/countries of interest is the FamilySearch wiki: **www.familysearch.org/wiki/en/Main_Page**

It has more than 91,000 genealogy topics worldwide that you can explore by place or record.

Typically the sorts of records you are looking for are:

- census records
- birth, marriage and death records
- newspapers
- Plus: electoral registers, phone books and trade directories, maps, military records, parish registers, passenger lists.

These are just a tiny selection of the many sorts of records that can be used for genealogy.

TIP! Get in to the habit of making a note of what you have looked at. This includes BOOKMARKING useful webpages (so that you don't lose that gem of a site you've found), and also creating a RESEARCH LOG.

- Genuki is full of useful UK and Ireland research information www.genuki.org.uk/
- FreeBMD, FreeCen & FreeReg have millions of free details about births, marriages and deaths, census returns & parish registers

WHAT DO YOU KNOW ALREADY?

As we've mentioned already, the golden rule is to start with yourself, then note down what you know about your parents and grandparents, and work backwards in time. Ask your family members what they know too. They may know names and dates you don't, and may have stories and photos to share.

Your research log

Your research log can be paper or digital. Set up a file with a few key columns:

- Date of research
- What & where you were researching
- What you found (and what you didn't find)
- What you want to find out next time

Need a hand setting up your research log? Head over to **www.family-tree.co.uk/information/fhwfb** and download your template research log

TIP! Get in the habit of learning about the record collections you use (whether online or in an archive). If you don't find your ancestor in a record collection you need to know whether this is because ...

a) the online collection isn't complete (and is a work in progress)

b) the archive collection isn't complete either (perhaps records were lost in a fire)

c) there are spelling mistakes/variations that you are not aware of and haven't searched for

d) Or is it that your ancestor really was never listed in that record collection?

For more tips and ideas to help you trace your family tree, see the Get Started section of the *Family Tree* website: https://www.family-tree.co.uk/getting-started

Question 3: Where can you create an online family tree?

As mentioned already in this *Workbook* there are numerous places to create a free online family tree. Examples include:

- FamilySearch
- Ancestry
- Findmypast
- MyHeritage
- TreeView
- Wikitree

Wherever you build your online tree it's important to think about protecting the privacy of living people. Most online trees will do this automatically (hiding living people from public view, so that only you, as the tree creator, can see them).

Have a think about photographs, stories and memories that you add to your online tree, however. These are not always automatically set to 'private' by the online tree providers. So, in order to be a best-practice family history researcher, you have a choice:

1. You can ask living relatives for permission to share items relating to them on your online tree.
2. You can set your entire tree to private (where settings of the online tree provider allow).
3. You can decide not to include such items in your online tree, and instead share them with family members another way.

We will cover in-depth steps to building your online tree later in the *Workbook* (see pages 32, 36 & 40).

Question 4: Will DNA help you?

Definitely yes. DNA will help you learn more about your family history. It will help you verify the family tree you are building and it will also be of vital assistance if you are seeking an unknown parent or grandparent, for instance. It is also extremely enjoyable to make connections with DNA matches – distant cousins with whom you may never have made contact otherwise.

As with all types of family history research, with DNA research you do need to be very aware that you may receive unexpected information about your relatives – or may find new relatives. If you were to receive such information you need to have a think about how you would feel, and if/how you might share such information with any relevant family members.

That said, for millions of people DNA testing is simply an excellent addition to the range of tools and resources that family historians use to trace their family trees.

What should I include in *my family history?*

What exactly is a family history and what should it include? Here we share some inspiration on creating a family history that's personal to you and can be passed down to the next generation with pride

WHAT IS A FAMILY HISTORY?

Very simply, a family history is the story of your family's past – collected and displayed in a way that's personal to you. There are no rules, and the project can be as simple or as extensive as you like. The story of your family is always changing and so this can be a long-term project that you build gradually over the years; easy to access history that you can share with family within a matter of days.

Read on for inspiration on what to include, how to put everything together, and the best ways to care for your family history treasures, from irreplaceable documents and photographs, to well-loved heirloom items that are still used in your home today.

Step 1: Assess what you have

Whether or not you know it, chances are you already have the makings of a family history, without needing to set foot outside the door. Old photographs, newspaper clippings, letters, diaries and certificates are examples of paper-based family history material to get you started.

As you begin, think about what's important to you and your family:

- Is the family history for your own use and enjoyment, or will you want to share it with others?
- Would you like to pass it down to the next generation?
- Do you want to commemorate an ancestor's military service?
- Or trace your maternal or paternal line back as far as you can?
- Perhaps you have deep roots in your local area and want to find out more about the history of your house and town?

Finding a 'peg' for the project is a good way to ensure you have a focus,will be researching topics that interest you and will help you make decisions about what to include.

Step 2: Time & space

Consider how much time you have to devote to the project, and where you might keep your family history. Although some items, such as old furniture and garden tools once owned by our ancestors might be in daily use, you will probably want to have your own collection of documents and photographs too, and perhaps scan some of your precious originals, both as a safeguard and to share with others.

Step 3: Online or offline?

Next, think about whether you'd like your family tree research to be online, offline or both. Obviously your original documents and photographs are offline items and we'll take a look at how to care for those in Step 4.

As you progress with your research, chances are that

Step 4: Caring for your family heirlooms

When it comes to storing paper-based documents and photographs, acid-free is the key! You can buy acid-free folders, boxes, tissue paper and photograph album pages from stationery stores. These have been designed to the standards used by archives and libraries for long-term storage.

Avoid storing any of your treasures in cold, damp spaces (such as the attic) or where they could be damaged by sunlight. Precious items such as war medals, clothing and china can also be stored in acid-free boxes and where practical, wrapped in archive-quality tissue paper to protect against dust.

Read our special home storage guide at **www.family-tree.co.uk/how-to-guides/how-to-care-for-family-tree-documents-at-home/**

you'll be doing a mixture of online research, and research carried out in archives, libraries and record offices, so have a think about how you'll record this information. If you like working on paper, then a collection of notebooks and a paper family tree chart would work well.

If you like the flexibility of digital, you can easily use a laptop or tablet, both at home and at record offices etc, keeping your notes organised and updating an online family tree as you work. FamilySearch **www.familysearch.org/en/** has a great free online family tree builder and commercial sites such as Ancestry, FindMyPast, MyHeritage and TheGenealogist all offer online trees and access to record collections that will help you trace your ancestors back in time.

Connect with others

Family history is more fun when you can share the ups and downs with others, not to mention the valuable knowledge available from people who've been researching for years, or who live in the same area that your ancestors did.

A great way to become part of the wider family history world is to join your local family history and/or the society that covers the area where your ancestors lived. Visit the Family History Federation for links to UK and overseas societies: **https://www.familyhistoryfederation.com/societies-az**

Step 5: Go way beyond names and dates

Family history is sometimes thought of as simply a collection of names and dates, but nothing could be further from the truth! You can bring the stories of your ancestors to life – and make things more interesting for yourself – by digging deeper.

Local newspapers, the census, old photographs, local histories and occupation records are just a few of the many ways in which you can put flesh on the bones of those names on your family tree. If you plan to share your

TOP 5 WEBSITES FOR GOING BEYOND NAMES AND DATES

❶ **The UK National Archives' alphabetical index of research guides** – from abbreviations to workhouse records **www.nationalarchives.gov.uk/help-with-your-research/research-guides-keywords/**

❷ **GENUKI** – UK and Ireland genealogy virtual reference library of family history links, directories and gazetteers: www.genuki.org.uk

❸ **Historical Directories** – discover the businesses, services, people, places and transport links of your ancestor's hometown over the years **https://specialcollections.le.ac.uk/digital/collection/p16445coll4**

❹ **A Vision of Britain Through Time** – explore Britain from 1801 onwards, with census reports, maps, statistical trends and an interactive map **https://www.visionofbritain.org.uk**

❺ **Commonwealth War Graves Commission** – Explore the register of war dead from the two World Wars to find out where your war-time military ancestor is buried **http://www.cwgc.org**

findings with family members, have a think about what might interest them too. Do you have a nurse in the family? Perhaps you can find an ancestor who served in the medical corps in one of the World Wars.

When it comes to those vital birth, marriage and death dates, think beyond that specific life. What was happening during those years? Which monarch was on the throne? Was there a strike, war, famine, or far-reaching historical event? Any of these might have impacted on your ancestor's life and as such, can be included as part of their life story.

Step 6: Who do you want to include?

As with the rest of this project, the question of who to include is very much up to you. In general, it's best to start with yourself and then work backwards, including your parents, grandparents, great-grandparents and so on.

If you prefer to work down just one of the lines – maternal or paternal – that's fine, and if you feel like a challenge, you can include the siblings of your parents and grandparents too.

Really don't forget to include yourself and present-day family. Keep labelled photographs, birth, marriage & death certificates and so on, to create your own future archive for your own descendants to enjoy.

Step 7: Sharing your family history

We hope that you'll enjoy working on your family history so much that it'll become a lifetime's work. A family history is never really complete – there's always something new to learn, new records to explore – and of course, your own life goes on, adding to the story of your family. So enjoy sharing your research with friends and relatives as you go.

Most online family tree providers have a facility to allow you to download your family history tree as a shareable file, or to share a weblink with others. You could even make copies of old photographs and documents for other family members. And don't forget to record the stories and memories of your aunts, uncles, cousins and grandparents too. If you're really lucky, they might have photos and documents that you haven't seen.

Enjoy making this project your own and connecting and sharing with others. We hope we've inspired you to start a project that will give you years of pleasure.

WHICH WEBSITE(S) DO I NEED? & DO I NEED TO PAY?

Discover useful ways to search free, dig deeper, and decide which of the fabulous paid for sites to subscribe to...
Here are some FAQs about paying, or not, for family history websites

Are there websites that will help me do my family history for free?

A Yes, plenty. As mentioned on pages 14-15 of the *Workbook* there are a number of websites with free access to essential clues. There are also a vast range of websites with free tools – such as those to help you:

- build your family tree online;
- download free charts and forms to keep your records straight;
- gather collections of photos of places from yesteryear;
- find historic maps;
- and read digitised old books.

There are also numerous wikis and online guides providing you with research advice and know-how to help you learn about how to trace your family tree, how to tackle advanced sources, how to overcome brickwalls and more.

But...

It can be well worth paying

A While you can do a lot without parting with a penny, many of the sites that do require paid-for access in order to view their collections will help you take your research to the next level. And this is why...

When searching the paid-for websites without a subscription, some clues will be revealed to you; however, by becoming a paid-up user you will be able to view greater details, and importantly be able to see the original historic digitised records too.

The following sites are all extremely valuable, particularly for British Isles family history, providing access to the essential records, further records to enhance your research, online tree building, ancestral matches and more:

- **www.ancestry.co.uk**
- **www.findmypast.co.uk**
- **www.myheritage.com**

- **www.thegenealogist.co.uk**
- **www.scotlandspeople.gov.uk**

To access the full information from any of these five websites above you will need to pay.

What should I look for when signing up to a website subscription?

A You'll definitely want to make sure they provide access to the census and BMDs.

- In addition have a think about collections you might wish to explore, as – in addition to the core records – the main sites mentioned above tend to have unique collections (not available on all the websites), such as various collections of newspapers, electoral rolls, DNA databases, tithe maps and more.
- Study the various subscription levels available to make sure the package you choose includes the datasets you need.
- Find out how the website allows you to contact fellow site users, and them you. Accessibility of contacting fellow researchers will help you trace new relations, ask questions and share findings.

Tip! If you have Scottish ancestors, then of the five, ScotlandsPeople.gov.uk is the website to use. It operates on a pay-per-view system (i.e. you buy credits, and use them as and when you wish to view a record). If you have paid access to Ancestry, it can be helpful to search the Scottish census indexes on Ancestry, find your ancestor, ensure you have the correct entry, and then pay to view the record on ScotlandsPeople. This will help you:

- make your search more accurate;
- may save you wasting credits on ScotlandsPeople;
- and will ensure you have the original record (from ScotlandsPeople – as Ancestry does not provide those for Scottish census returns).

What should a newbie look for when signing up to a paid website?

A The websites mentioned above will all allow you to build and grow an online tree and search the key records. If you're new to family history it's worth taking advantage of any free trial periods so that you can explore each site and see which suits you best.

Can you tell me the must-search FREE websites?

A There sites are some that you should certainly search. We recommend bookmarking them in your browser so that you can easily find them when doing your family history.

In addition to those mentioned on pages 14-15 of the *Workbook*, see also:

- **www.irishgenealogy.ie** – for Irish civil BMD records and some parishes
- **www.census.nationalarchives.ie** – for Irish 1901 and 1911 Censuses
- **www.library.wales/collections/learn-more/introduction2/** – for a wealth of Welsh digital records (you'll wish you had Welsh ancestors)
- **https://scotlandsplaces.gov.uk** – a treasure trove of information, photos and documents for tracing ancestors in Scotland.
- *See page 46 for further coverage of archive websites, many of which provide a selection of free online digitised collections.*

Am I missing out if I just do my family history for free?

A Yes, you may be.

While there is a huge amount you can accomplish for free, paying for records really is worth it to enrich your research and give you access to digitised documents, to help you trace the full facts from the original sources, for more detailed, credible research.

If you happen to live near the archives for the area in which your ancestors came from you will be able to achieve a lot using the archival collections. Many people

live far from the localities in which their ancestors lived, so archive trips are more difficult to accomplish.

In addition many archives and local libraries offer free access to certain subscription sites to their visitors or members.

I've been doing family history for a year or two, what should I look out for in a paid website?

A With a year or two's experience, you'll be very familiar with the key records, so it's really worth looking at the data collections of each site before paying out.

Find further information about each site's collections at:

- **https://search.ancestry.co.uk/search/CardCatalog.aspx**
- **https://search.findmypast.co.uk/historical-records/**
- **www.myheritage.com/research**
- **www.thegenealogist.co.uk/diamond**

I've done quite a bit of work on my family tree, is there any way I can upload this to an online tree?

A If you have created a paper-based family tree you are going to need to key in the details in order to create your online family tree.

However, if you have a digital copy of your family tree (for instance passed on to you by a family member and created using family history software, or perhaps one you have created yourself using such software), you can easily upload it to many of the websites that provide tree-builing. In order to do this you need to upload a GEDCOM.

Tip! The ability to import (upload) and export (download) your family tree is extremely useful (saving you from reinventing the wheel. If uploading your research to the paid website, you can very often still have access to it should you wish to cease subscribing. Look out for the ability to 'Import GEDCOM' or 'Export GEDCOM' on your website of choice.

I'm thinking about taking a DNA test, which site should I subscribe to?

A Explore each website's DNA options. Ideally you need a website with the largest database of fellow testers, to maximise your chance of making connections.

DNA testing websites that provide tools to help you organise and analyise your DNA test results are also extremely useful.

For family historians Ancestry, MyHeritages, FamilyTreeDNA and 23andMe each tick many of these boxes.

• *See pages 90, 94 & 96 of the Workbook for further information on working with DNA test results.*

KEEP A LIST OF WHAT YOU WISH TO RESEARCH

We all know that it's important to watch your spending. You may not wish to subscribe to a website month after month. These two tips will help you focus your time and money.

1. Remember to keep records of your research. One of your records may be a list of the records that you wish to search when you have a paid-for subscription. See the Workbook hub page for a downloadable Records Wish List to download and fill in.
2. Check with your local library: some libraries offer their members free access at the library to websites such as Ancestry and Findmypast.

HOW TO BOOKMARK A WEB PAGE

Bookmarking a web page isn't a tactic that's specific to family history is it, but it is one that will come in extremely useful. As you will have noticed on reading the *Workbook* so far, there are some websites that we mention time and time again. Very likely you'd find it useful to bookmark them so that you can easily return to them later. Conversely, sometimes when doing family history you will come across a little-known site – that has just the information you need... if so you need to bookmark. It's extremely frustrating, not being able to find a website again, so don't put yourself in that position – if you find something, bookmark it. Here are some tips to bookmarking web pages with Google Chrome. Other browsers also offer bookmarking facilities.

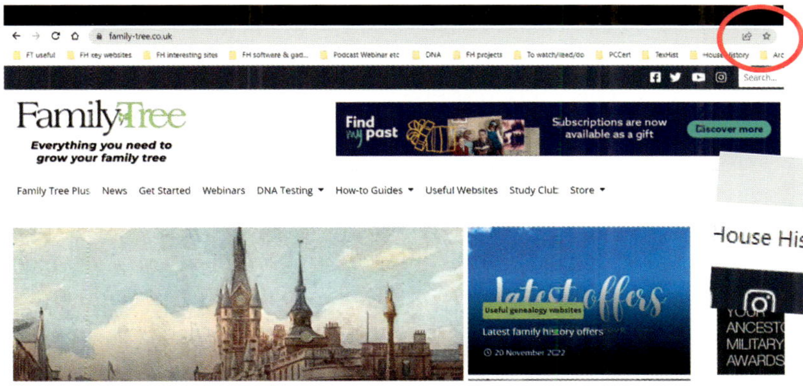

Step 1: Go to a website you wish to bookmark. Here we have chosen www.family-tree.co.uk

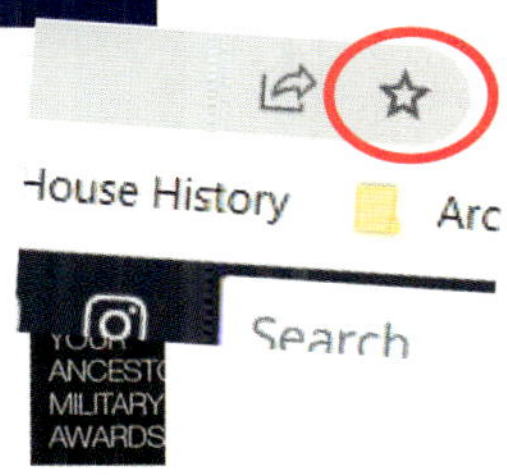

Step 2: To bookmark the page, simply click on the star in the top right-hand corner of the window.

Once you've bookmarked it, it will turn blue.

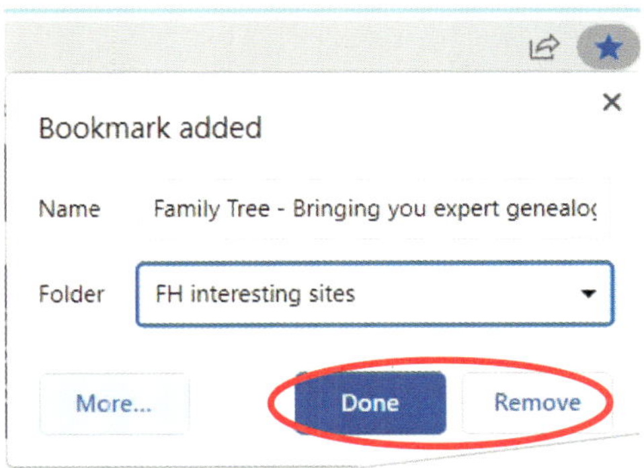

Step 3: Over time you're likely to find many family history websites and web pages of interest. So you may find it helpful to create folders for your bookmarks. Then as you come across more you can add them to the relevant folder.

When you click the star to bookmark it, the options window (shown left) will appear. You can drop your bookmark into an existing folder, or click on 'More' to create a new one.

Press 'Done' – and that's it.

While you're here, note the 'Remove' button – useful to know in case you change your mind in the future.

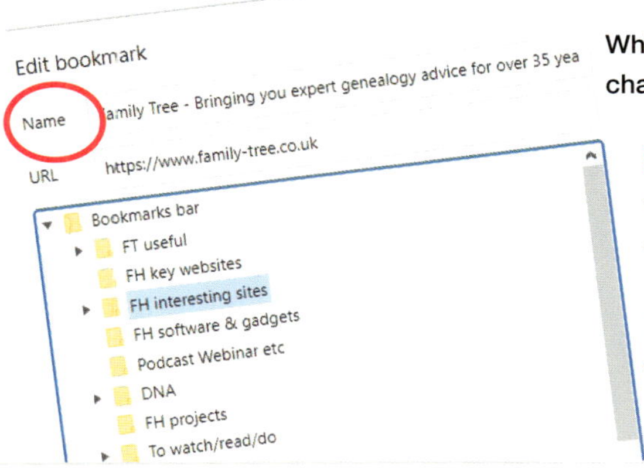

Step 4: Just as with the folders on your computer, you can create sub-folders. You may want to create a folder for each of the surnames, places, or old occupations that you're investigating.

Note that at any time you wish, you can edit the name of the webpage to something more useful to you. Just retype in the name box.

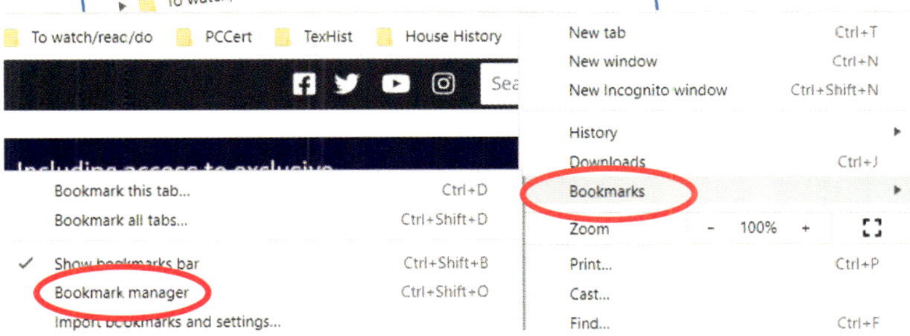

Step 5: One last tip! If you feel as though your bookmarks have got in a jumble and wish to rearrange them, go to the three grey dots (top right of your Google Chrome browser window), from the drop-down menu select 'Bookmarks' then 'Bookmark manager'.

YOUR GO-TO SUBSCRIPTION/PAID SITES

Explore go-to genealogy websites to discover what's out there to help you

There are billions of family history records online for you to explore, and keeping up to date with what's available can be a challenge. Explore the subscription sites below and the features we've highlighted which will help you keep up to speed, so that you don't miss out on useful records for tracing your family tree. This page is all about learning how to explore which resources the key paid family history websites have to help you.

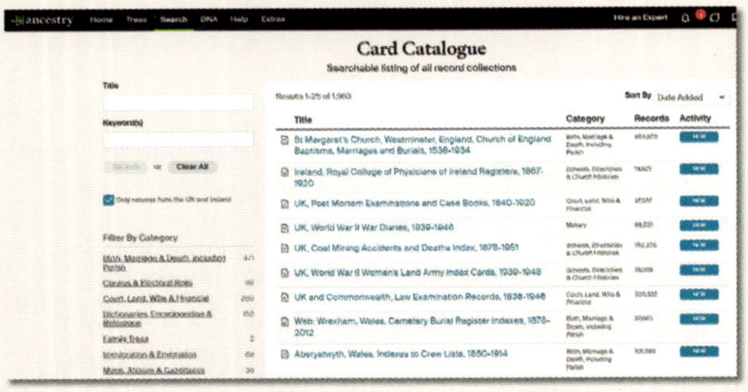

Ancestry.co.uk

To see newly updated collections visit the dedicated page at **www.ancestry.co.uk/cs/recent-collections**

To explore Ancestry's comprehensive listing of all the site's resources, see **https://search.ancestry.co.uk/search/cardcatalog.aspx**

- [ ] Yes I've explored the site
- [ ] Yes I've looked at the Search Tips and Search Resources at **https://support.ancestry.co.uk/s/search-and-records**

Notes of collections of interest:

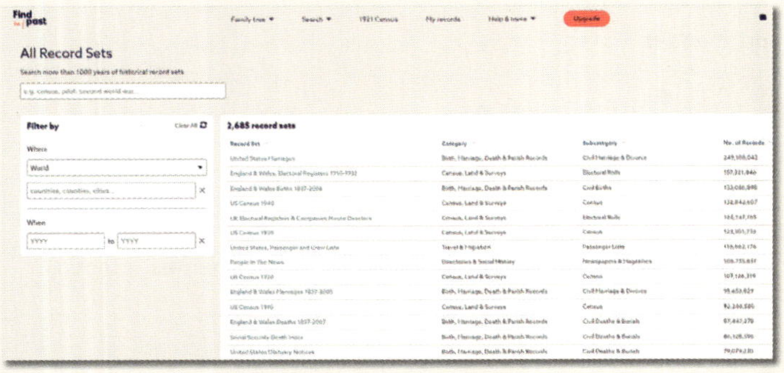

Findmypast.co.uk

To see the full collections available from around the world, view the A to Z listings: **https://search.findmypast.co.uk/historical-records**

Keep up with the latest releases at **https://www.findmypast.co.uk/blog/new**

- [ ] Yes I've explored the site
- [ ] Yes I've explored the Help Hub at **www.findmypast.co.uk/blog/help**

Notes of collections of interest:

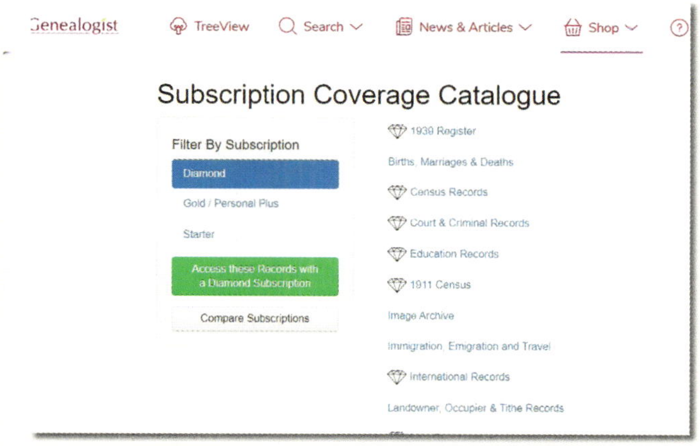

TheGenealogist.co.uk

For the latest site releases see **www.thegenealogist.co.uk/news/#latest**

To see what's available via the different subscription tiers, see **www.thegenealogist.co.uk/coverage**

☑ Yes I've explored the site

☑ Yes I've looked at the Research Guide at **www.thegenealogist.co.uk/researchguide/**

Notes of collections of interest:

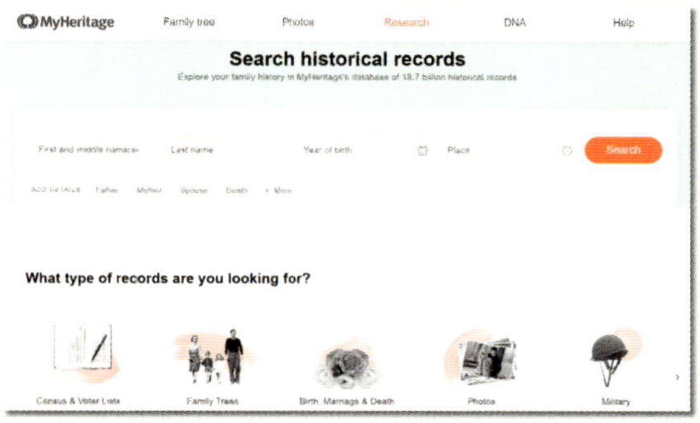

MyHeritage.com

Get an idea of the 9 billion worldwide records at **www.myheritage.com/research**

To see the latest record releases, keep an eye at **https://blog.myheritage.com/category/historical-records**

☑ Yes I've explored the site

☑ Yes I've looked at the overview of historic collections at **www.myheritage.com/research**

Notes of collections of interest:

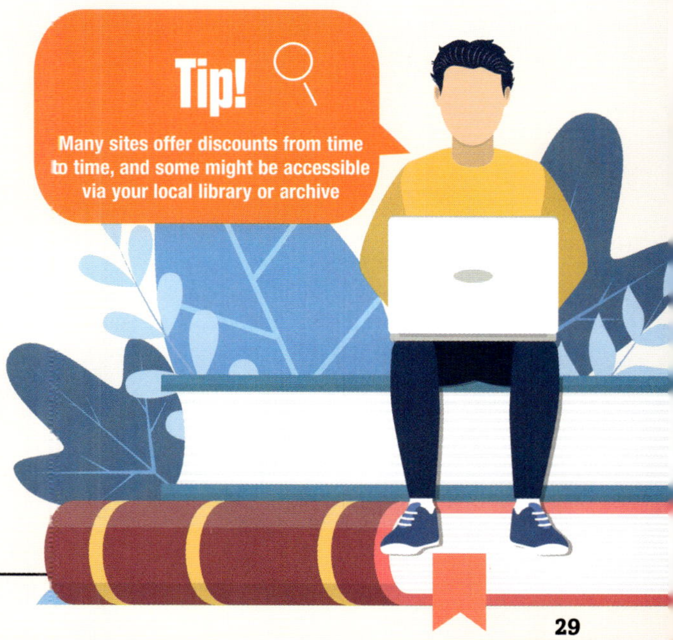

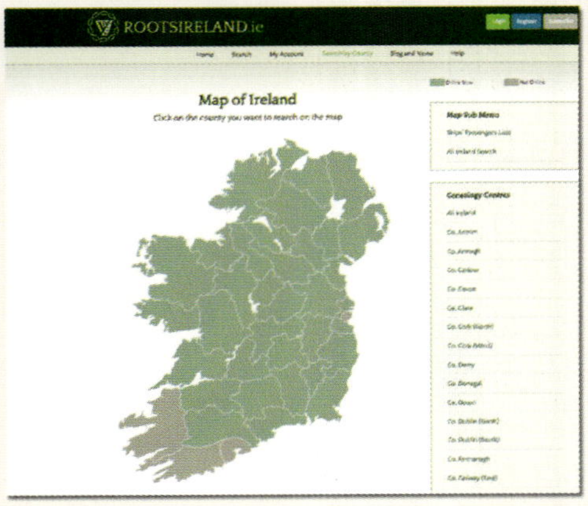

RootsIreland.ie

Explore the 21 million records on the site via the map at **www.rootsireland.ie/map**

☑ Yes I've explored the site

☑ Yes I've explored the guides at **www.rootsireland.ie/help/help-getting-started/**

Notes of collections of interest:

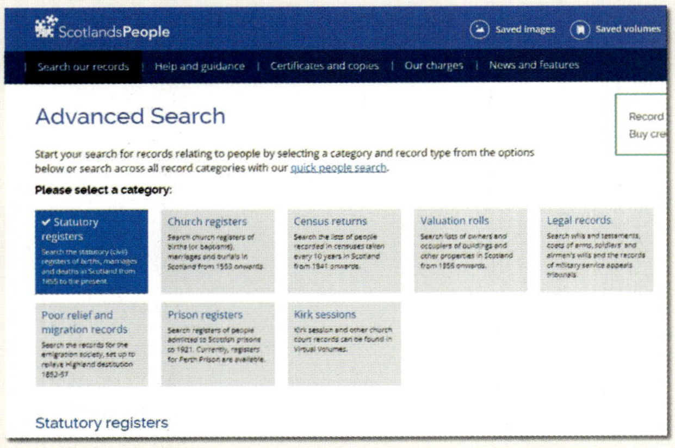

Scotlandspeople.gov.uk

To explore an overview of the records available see **www.scotlandspeople.gov.uk/advanced-search**

☑ Yes I've explored the site

☑ Yes I've looked at the guides to the records at **www.scotlandspeople.gov.uk/guides**

Notes of collections of interest:

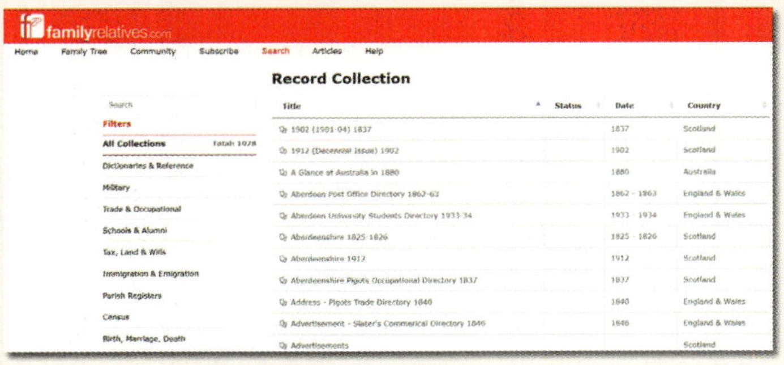

FamilyRelatives.com

See the collections available at **www.familyrelatives.com/post_search.php**

☑ Yes I've explored the site

Notes of collections of interest:

Register

Many of these sites will require you to register (free) in order to be able to search more fully; then pay in order to view more details or original records

Guidance!

Many of these sites provide how-to guides giving you useful background information to the records

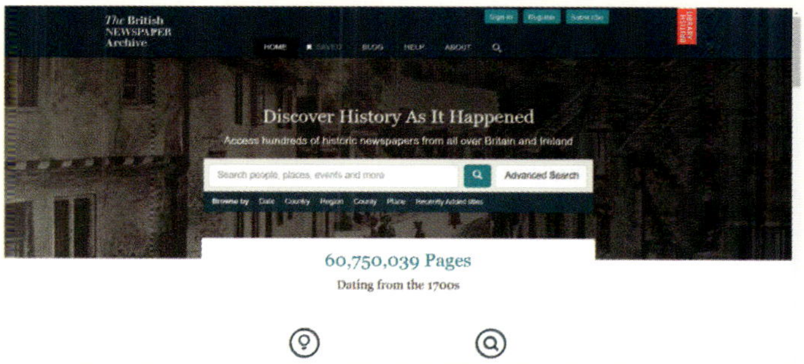

BritishNewspaperArchive.co.uk

See the collections available at
www.britishnewspaperarchive.co.uk

☐ Yes I've explored the site

Notes of collections of interest:

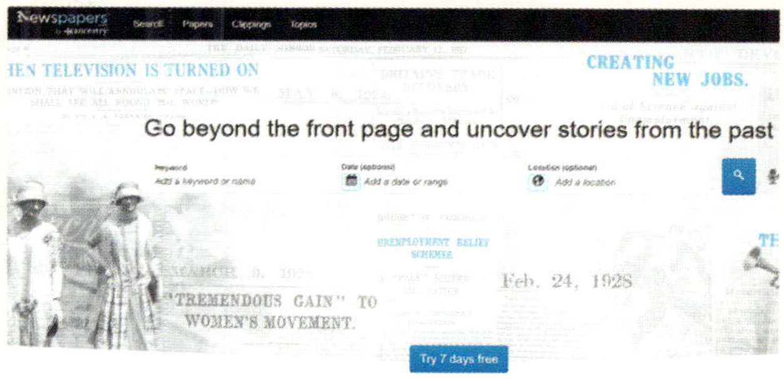

Newspapers.com

See the collections available at
www.newspapers.com

☐ Yes I've explored the site

Notes of collections of interest:

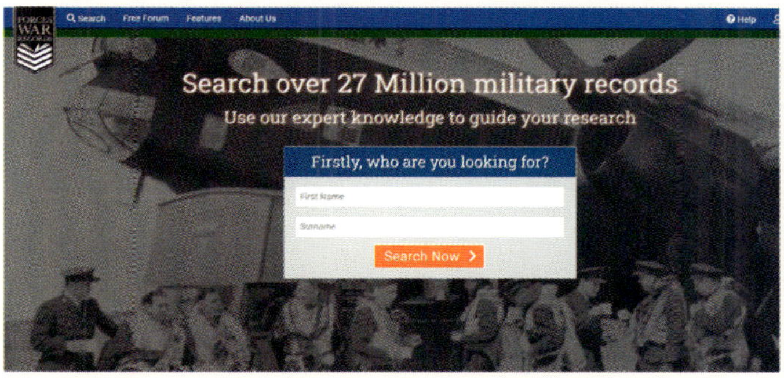

Forces-War-Records.co.uk

See the collections available at
forces-war-records.co.uk/collections

☐ Yes I've explored the site

Notes of collections of interest:

Fold3.com

See the collections available at
www.fold3.com/browse

☐ Yes I've explored the site

Notes of collections of interest:

Dos & don'ts of building an ONLINE FAMILY TREE

Here we're going to look at some of the key dos & don'ts when it comes to building your online family tree, to help ensure that yours is a great tree with strong roots in solid research

First steps

When first starting your online tree, follow the advice that we covered on the how to get started (see page 18) and what to include (see page 20). This means starting with yourself, and working backwards in time, gradually adding details to your tree, as and when you have found clues and evidence, so that you can be sure that the details you're adding really are those of *your* ancestor (not just someone with the same name etc).

✦ THE BASICS ✦

There are many different websites to choose from, on which to build your online family tree and many of them are free to use.

Such online trees are an extremely valuable family history tool enabling you to:

- access your research wherever you are
- collaborate and compare notes with fellow family researchers
- add photos and pictures of memorabilia, enabling you to create an online archive to share with family
- and include documentation, notes and sources, helping you to keep your research organised and provable.

What NOT to do & what TO do

It can be really tempting to use the auto-prompts (aka the 'hints'), which may be provided with the website you use, to grow your tree rapidly. However, you will thank yourself and avoid a muddle if – rather than accepting every hint – you progress carefully, ensuring that each piece of information is correct before adding another detail to your tree.

It can also be tempting to copy information from other people's online trees – especially if it seems that there are numerous people all with that same information on their tree. While of course it can be interesting to look at other people's family trees, we advise conducting your own research for several reasons, so that:

1. you can ensure it is correct
2. you have proof of which source provided you with the clue
3. and you grow your own family history knowledge and search skills, by doing it yourself.

Note: You can always reach out to other people, with whom it seems you share ancestors, and ask whether they are happy to share research insights with you. Two heads may be better than one, and together you can solve problems on your family trees. Plus you have the enjoyment of a new friend and/or relation.

ONLINE TREES

All the major family history record collection sites (Ancestry, Findmypast, MyHeritage, TheGenealogist, FamilySearch) allow you to create an online family tree free of charge.

Consider your sources

Sources are the proof of your research, providing evidence of your research steps and deductions.

When you are searching for your ancestor online you may see that the search results return a mixture of items:

• some will be original records for you to follow up (such as census entries);

• and others will be entries in other people's family trees.

Both items are valuable and interesting to look at, but if you skip the original records and solely rely on other people's trees you not only risk unwittingly including errors in your own tree, you also miss the pleasure and satisfaction of studying the original documents yourself. Most of these will be records created in your ancestors' own times.

By studying the originals you may spot additional clues of interest that the other people haven't noted in their research. A witness's name on a marriage certificate, for example, or one of the neighbour's names on a census page may be that of someone you know to be another relation. Thus it really is so valuable to study the original records in person yourself.

Keep those great notes

You will hopefully make many discoveries as you search for and build your tree online. Keeping great notes and adding them to your tree is the most time-efficient, effective and thorough way to work. Set yourself up to be an excellent family history researcher by keeping good notes and providing sources on your family tree. Do this by:

• Saving a copy of the digitised document that has provided you with the information. You can save it to your online tree and/or to a folder on your computer.

• Making a note to yourself of where you found the information. This will enable you and anyone with whom you share your research, to track down the record again.

• Writing down why you think your finding is correct.

As you will be gathering information about so many ancestors when you do your family history, you'll soon

Search widely

If you are keen to find living relations, then search other family trees and other websites for shared ancestral connections – as a distant cousin may be building their tree on a different platform to you

realise that you can get in a muddle if you don't keep good notes. Good notes also mean that you will be able to revisit your research and pick up where you left off, even if a little time has elapsed.

Public or private?

While many of our vital details – birthdays, addresses, and more – are readily available online, we would always advise that it is good etiquette not to publish the details of living people in your online family tree without their permission. (To be safe, we would advise that you don't publish their details).

Many online tree-building websites ask you to specify whether someone is 'alive' or 'deceased'; the websites then privatise the details of living people automatically. Some trees allow you to choose whether to privatise your entire tree.

The decision as to how public to be is up to you. Sharing your tree publicly allows others to see your research, thus you can collaborate, perhaps find distant kin, share solutions to common problems, swap copies of family photos and more.

There is no right or wrong approach, but if you would like to protect your research perhaps the answer is to just publish part of your research online.

Media, memories

Very often the photos, documents, and perhaps audio and video files, that can be attached to online family trees are referred to as 'media'. On FamilySearch pictures and audio clips are referred to as 'memories.'

If you opt to have your tree public then you will find that your material is readily available to others, findable via the website's search system. Many online family tree websites tend to actively encourage people to share such photos and incorporate them into their own family trees.

This is not at all wrong – indeed it provides a useful and fascinating addition to our research, enabling us to see pictures of ancestors that we might never get to see otherwise. It is just worth knowing: if you are going to add your photos etc to your online tree, unless you set your tree to private (where possible), then expect that other people will be able to access, use and copy these photos etc too.

Note too that in some instances – even when your tree is set to private, and even if a photo depicts a living person – those photos may nevertheless be publicly viewable. You may not mind this, but it is worth understanding, particularly as your relations may have different views on an acceptable level of visibility.

Secondly, if you are going to use other people's photos in a context other than your online tree (for instance on your blog, or a family history book you may be writing) it could be diplomatic to ask their permission, giving them credit as to the ownership of the original where relevant. There are two key considerations to bear in mind: one is copyright and the other is courtesy.

Creating a back-up

If you are happy to share all your research online, we would still recommend keeping a copy of your findings on your computer, by way of a back-up. MyHeritage will automatically send you a back-up of your research and family tree on their site on a monthly basis. If not using MyHeritage you can set a reminder to create your own regular back-ups.

Be GEDCOM savvy

GEDCOM is a type of file, specific to genealogy, which allows people to transport their research from one platform to another. For instance, you may wish to export your research from your family history computer software, and upload it to create an online family tree. Alternatively you may wish to export your online family tree as a GEDCOM, so that you can get a giant family tree chart printed, for instance from **www.my-history.co.uk**.

When creating your online tree, look out for the option to import and export GEDCOM files as this will save you time and trouble. Where GEDCOM isn't an option there can be workarounds. FamilySearch for instance doesn't provide the facility for you to export your tree as a GEDCOM. However, you can access your FamilySearch tree via some family history software programs, such as Family Tree Maker, download it and export it as a GEDCOM file.

Link your tree to your DNA

If you have taken a DNA test and the website provides the facility to add and link your family tree, be sure to do this. This will enable your DNA matches to view your tree and see how you may be connected.

To find out more about using DNA with your family history see page 90 of the Workbook.

Your online tree

We have written throughout about your online tree in the singular. You may of course wish to have multiple trees. Great reasons for creating multiple trees are:

- the quick and dirty trees favoured by DNA family historians (who create private family trees on which to record their work-in-progress research)
- a surprise family tree dedicated to the ancestry of a relative to commemorate a special date or event
- the family tree of someone not related to you, but who is the subject of your house history, or a book you're writing, say.

Some websites will allow you to create multiple trees – so where this facility exists make use of it.

It's extremely easy to create your family tree online and great fun too. We hope that these tips will help you benefit from all the advantages of having an online family tree for efficient, enjoyable research, and maximise your chances of making connections with distant kin too.

START AN ONLINE TREE ON ANCESTRY

STEP-BY-STEP

It's totally free to build online family trees using Ancestry. Follow these steps to discover the tree-building tools

1

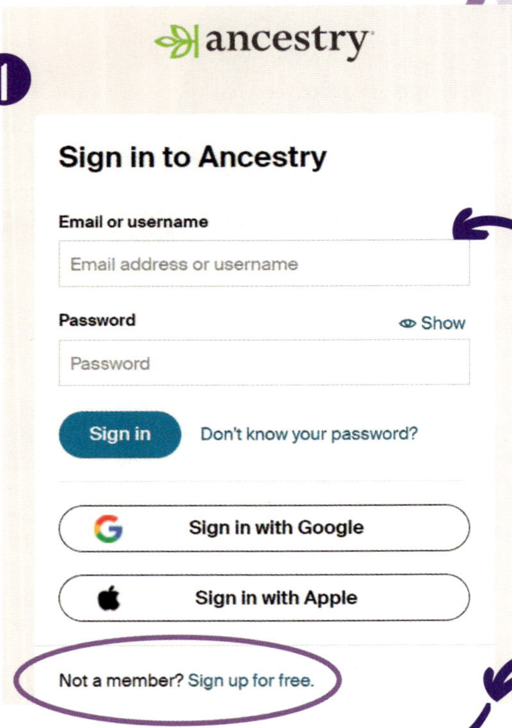

To start a new online family tree at Ancestry go to www.ancestry.co.uk You'll then be invited to sign in; if you've not yet created an Ancestry account, scroll down to 'Sign up for free'.

VIDEO GUIDE

Turn to page 55 to discover how to view a video guide to building a family tree on Ancestry.co.uk

2

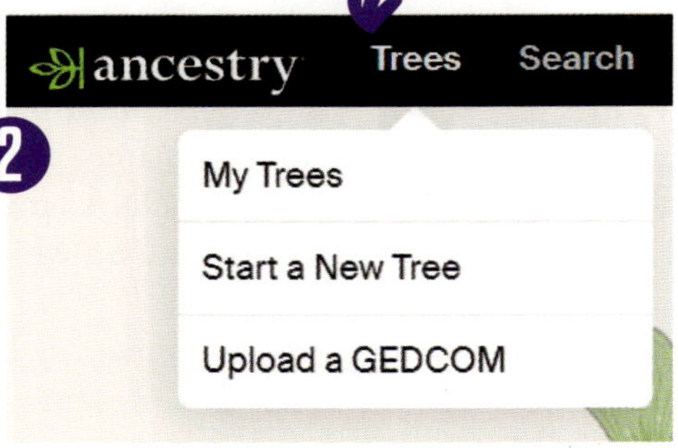

To get to the tree-building tools, select 'Trees' from the black bar, select your preferred option from the drop-down menu:

- 'My Trees' – here you will find the trees you have already created; over time you may wish to create several family trees.
- 'Start a New Tree' – this is the option you are most likely to wish to use.
- 'Upload a GEDCOM' – a GEDCOM is a specific type of genealogy file which enables family historians to transfer family trees from one platform or piece of software to another. If you are just starting family history you won't have a GEDCOM, but it may be that a relation has gifted you their research in the form of a GEDCOM file. If so this is where you can upload it and view it on Ancestry.

3

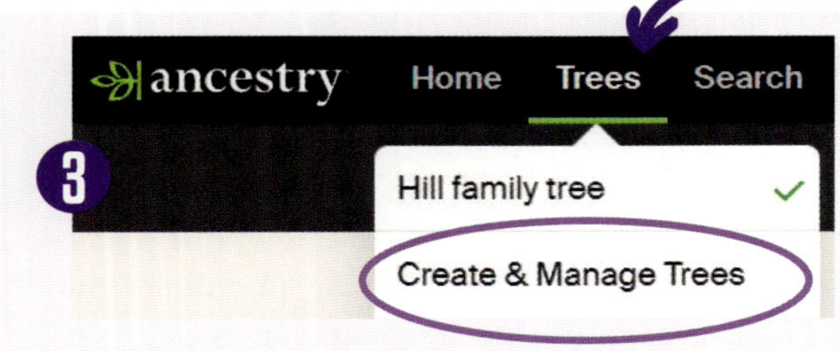

If you've already begun creating a tree on Ancestry in the past, you'll find it listed in 'Trees'. If you wish to start a new one, select 'Create & Manage Trees'.

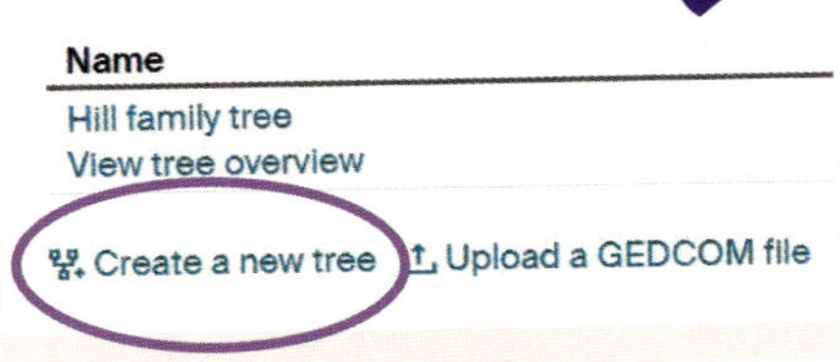

The window, shown left, will appear: providing links to allow you to view your existing tree(s), to 'Upload a GEDCOM', or to 'Create a new tree'. That's the one we're going to select today: 'Create a new tree'.

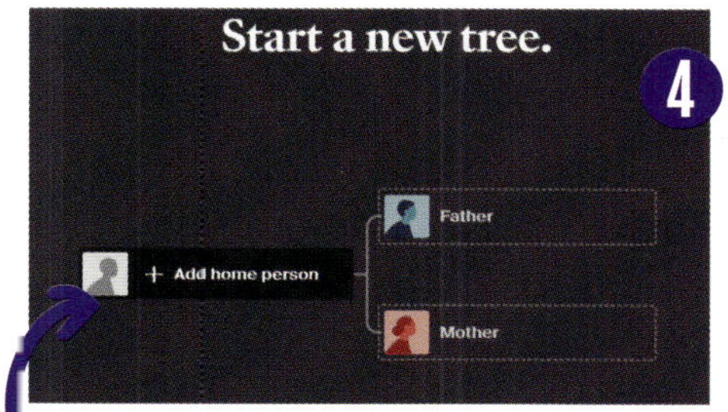

Now you can start building your tree. You can start with yourself as the Root Person of the tree; or start with any other relative of your choosing. You can of course build family trees for your friends too.

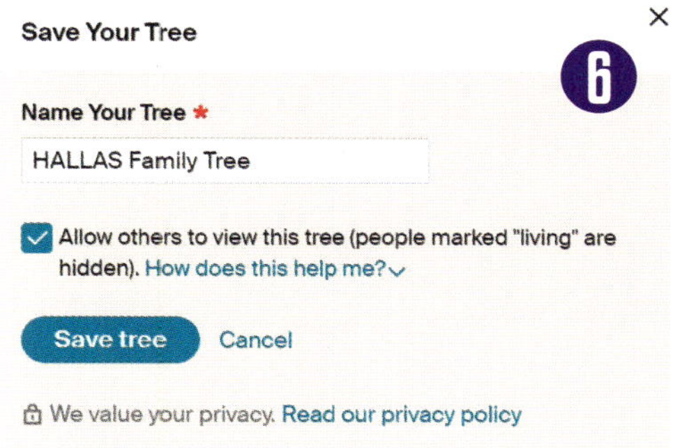

You will be prompted to name your family tree and to save it. The default is for the box to be ticked to allow others to view your tree. To learn more about tree settings, see number 13.

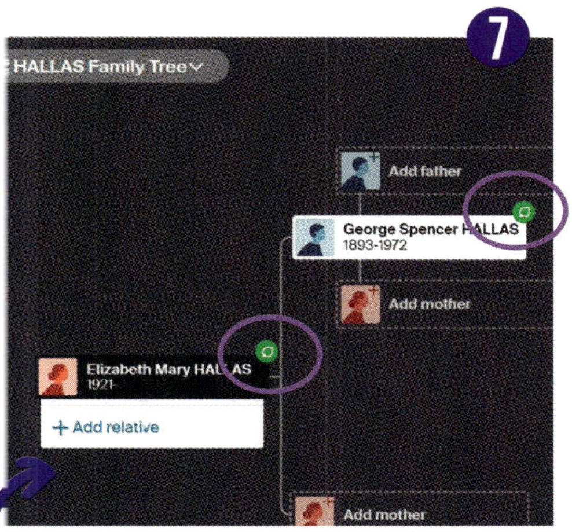

Even with a tiny tree, you will soon notice that green leaves appear on your tree, providing auto-hints to possible clues about your ancestors. The hints may be to records in the Ancestry collections or to photos or mentions in other people's family trees on Ancestry that contain someone by the same name as your ancestor.

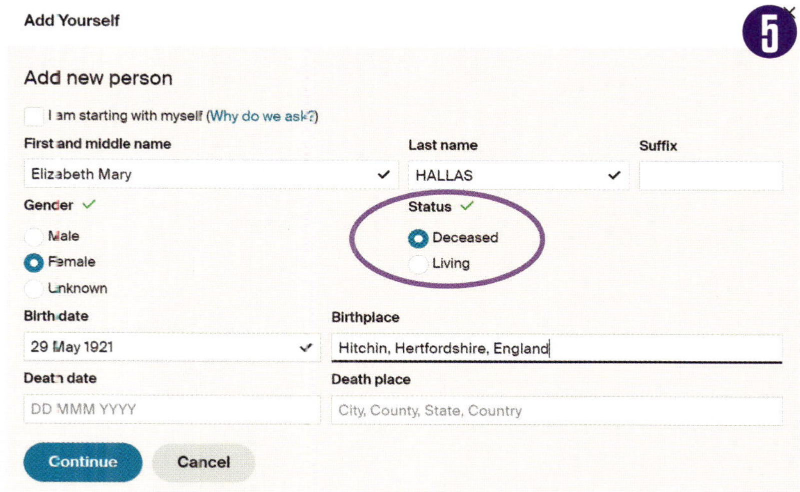

In this example, the person is not starting with themselves; instead they are starting the tree with a deceased ancestor. The fields to fill in are self-explanatory. An important point to note is to be careful to ensure that people are correctly defined as living or deceased. You need to ensure that all people still living are marked 'living'. Doing so will keep their details private: *you* will be able to see their details (as will anyone with whom you decide to share your tree) but to anyone else their details will be privatised.

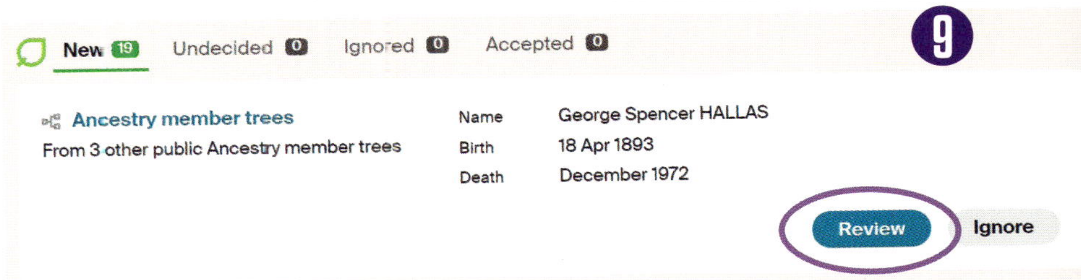

If you are currently on a 14-day free trial with Ancestry, or if you have taken out a paid membership you will be able to view further details. If not, when you click 'Review', you will find that you can see some details, but others are blurred out (as shown in number 10 below) or otherwise in accessible.

10 Without seeing the full details it can be hard to determine whether the record relates to your ancestor. We would advise that you look at hints solely as an additional tactic to find out further records about a known ancestor, and not as the means to build your tree.

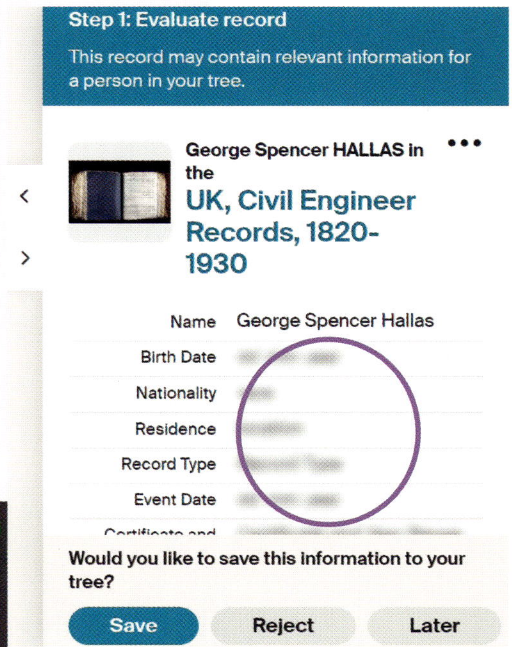

Select someone on your tree, and click the leaf. Here we can see that there are 19 hints for George.

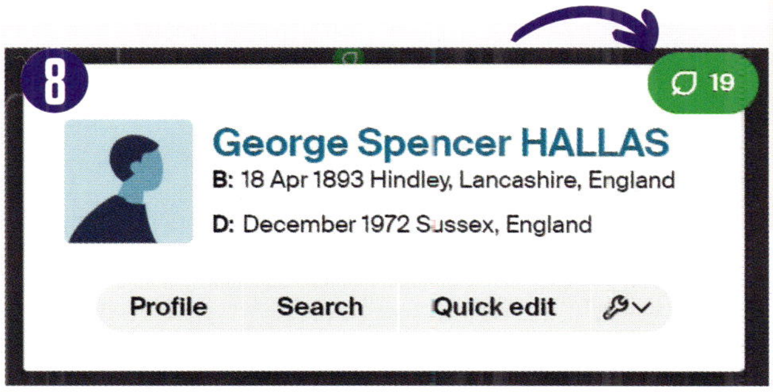

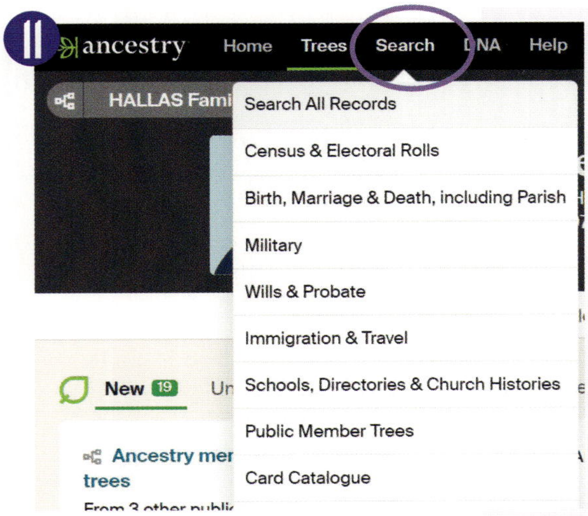

Rather than relying on the hints, we recommend that you search for clues about your ancestors yourself and work methodically through the records, starting with the root person on your tree, and working backwards in time. As mentioned elsewhere in the *Workbook*, records such as the census, births, marriages and deaths and parish registers are key collections to search for ancestors in. Ancestry provides very good access to many of these records.

Where else can you find clues?

- It could be that you have family papers (e.g. newspaper clippings, birthday books, marriage certificates, Army service records etc) at home. If so you can use these details to build your family tree on Ancestry.
- If you don't have paid access to Ancestry, then see page 14 of the *Workbook* for useful free websites.

Clicking on someone on your family tree will bring up their profile.

The **LifeStory** narrative is generated automatically, but by clicking 'edit' you can amend it and add to it in your own words.

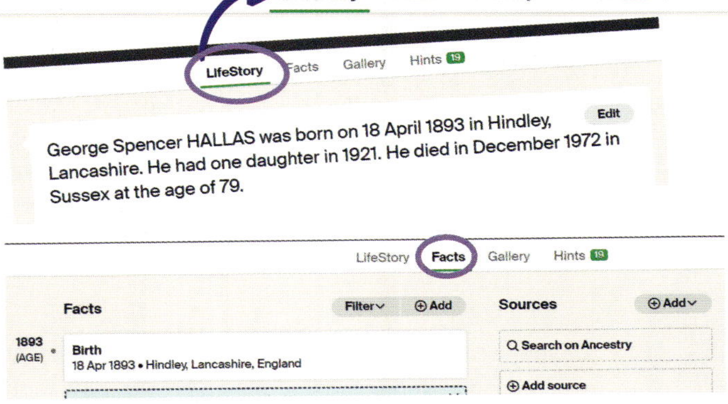

The **Facts** window shows a timeline of details, and links to the sources that you've added. For further info about the importance of sources, and how to use them on Ancestry, see page 9 of the *Workbook*.

Note the 'edit' button, using which you can edit the details you've entered about the person, and more. **Tip!** All the details you enter on your Ancestry tree can be easily edited, so if you make a mistake don't worry as you can easily put it right.

The **Gallery** reveals media (these can be copies of your family photos or documents that you've found on Ancestry for instance) that you have added to that ancestor.

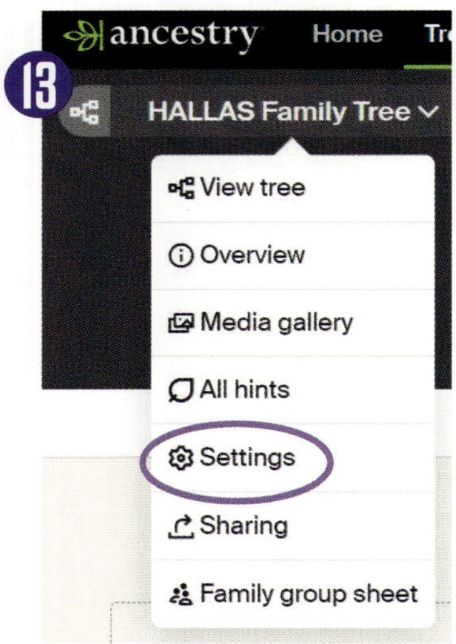

There are a few ways to locate the tree **Settings**; one way is to select 'Settings' from the drop-down menu from your tree name, while viewing your tree.

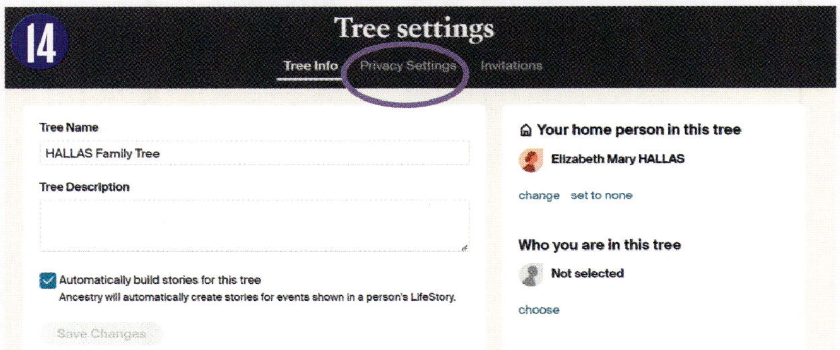

From here, in **Tree Settings**, you can edit the tree name, change the home person in the tree, adjust your hint preferences, and also find 'Privacy Settings'. In 'Privacy Settings' you can opt to make your tree public, private or private and unsearchable. Note that if you make your tree public then it can help a relation to find you. Note too that family photos you upload to Ancestry will be publicly viewable if your tree is viewable, even if the person they depict is still alive.

Is it worth paying for Ancestry? Having paid access to Ancestry will make your research vastly more productive and interesting, providing you with full access to the record collections you opt to pay for: memberships start from £10.99 per month for UK essentials, £13.99 per month UK Premium, and £19.99 per month UK Worldwide.

PRIZES WORTH £199!

WIN! A ONE-YEAR ANCESTRY WORLDWIDE SUBSCRIPTION

We have Ancestry one-year worldwide subscriptions to give away to two lucky winners in this exclusive competition. That's 12 months access to UK, Ireland & all International records on Ancestry.

For your chance to win just head over to the *Family Tree* website, answer the following question, and be sure to sign up to receive the free *Family Tree* newsletter:

Which British monarch was on the throne when the 1841 census was taken?

COMPETITION TERMS Worldwide membership includes access to UK, Ireland & all International records on Ancestry. The two winners will be picked at random from all correct entries. Closing date: 31 March 2023. Editor's decision is final. For full competition terms see: www.warnersgroup.co.uk/competition-terms. Good luck!

ENTER NOW FOR YOUR CHANCE TO WIN:

WWW.FAMILY-TREE.CO.UK/COMPETITIONS

Start an online tree on FamilySearch

STEP-BY-STEP

There are many options to choose from when creating an online family tree. Here we're going to explore the FamilySearch Family Tree which is freely available. Note – you can also explore millions of free records on FamilySearch too, covering family history from all over the world.

1

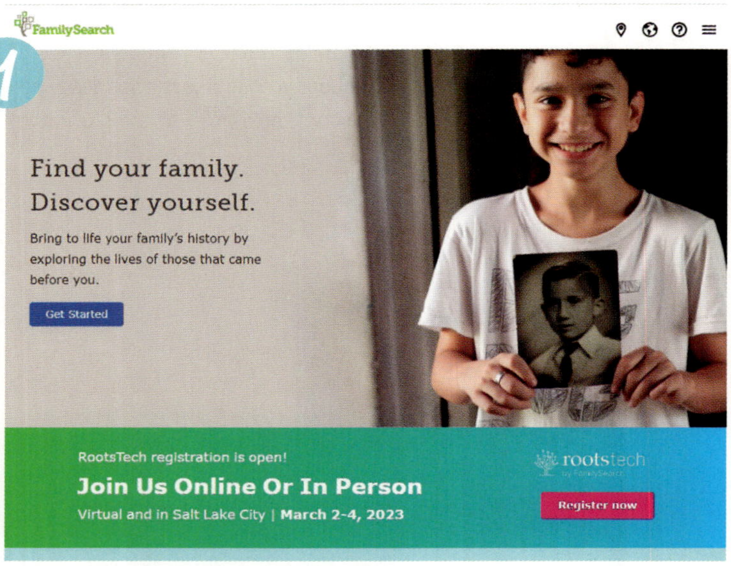

Register your account at www.familysearch.org. Start your tree with yourself, adding children, siblings, parents etc. The details of all living people will only be visible to you; the details of the deceased will be publicly available. With each person you add to your tree, you define them as alive or deceased.

2

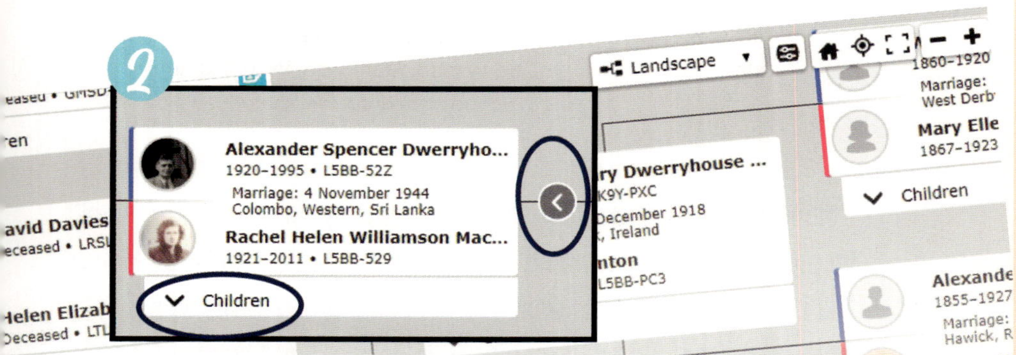

Gradually fill in the vital biographical details for each member of your family tree and watch the family network grow. Use the arrows to navigate to earlier generations, and note that you can find the children for each couple easily using the drop-down menu.

A COLLABORATIVE FAMILY TREE

The FamilySearch Family Tree is collaborative, as it aims to create one vast global online tree. This means that you will be able to benefit from other people's research: e.g. discoveries about your shared ancestors that they have made. It also means that people can change, correct and add to each other's entries.

VIDEO GUIDE

Turn to page 55 to discover how to view a video guide to building a family tree on FamilySearch

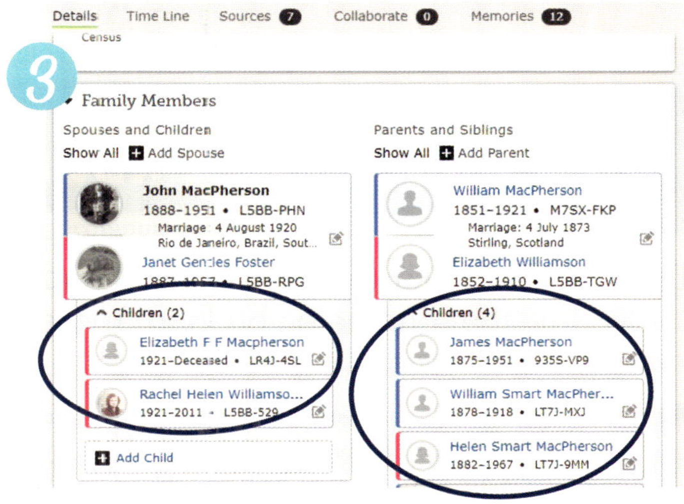

In the example above you can see that a few children have been added for each couple. Including the details of as many ancestors as possible in this way (not **just** your direct ancestors) will help you make connections with distant relations. For instance you may find a fellow FamilySearch user who is descended from your 2x great-aunt – and this descendant may have useful information to share!

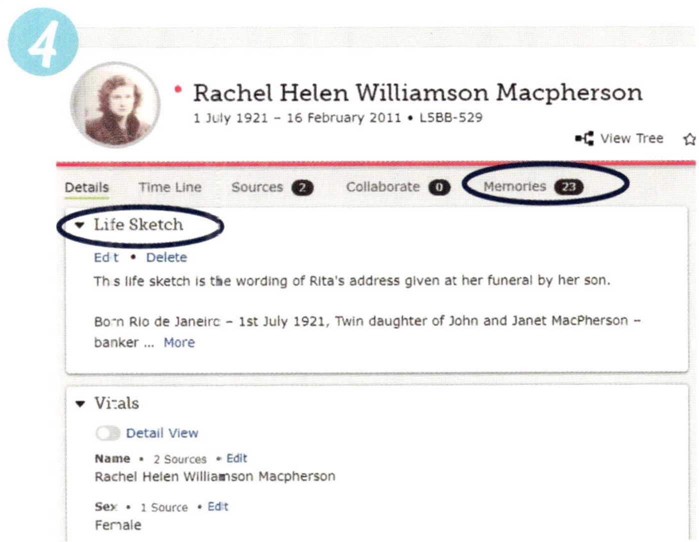

As you find out more, include a 'life sketch' for each ancestor – this is the space in which you can 'tell their life story', which other relations may be interested to read. Memories, including audio recordings, and photos can be added via the 'Memories' tab.

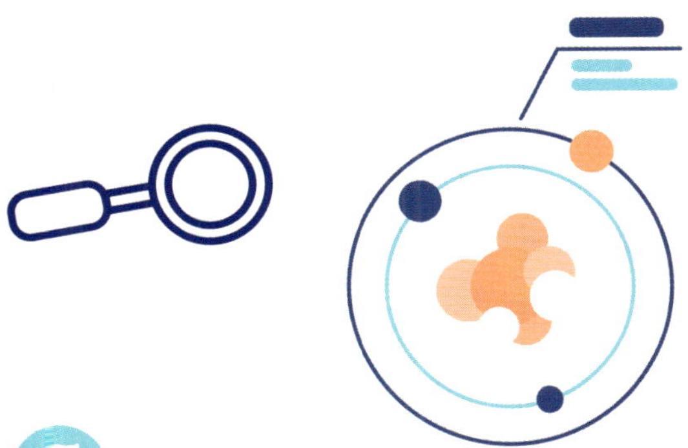

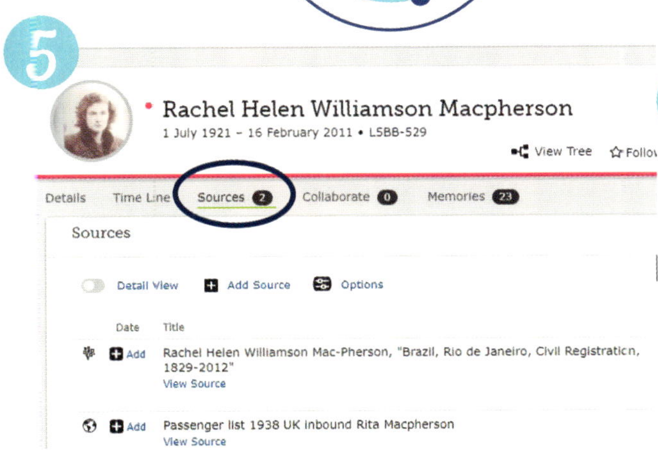

Try to remember to include 'sources' – these help to verify the reliability of your research. This person has added 23 memories but only 2 sources – something to build on!

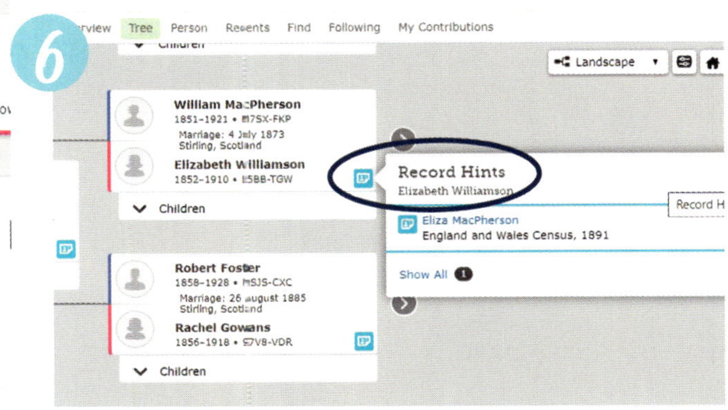

Click on the blue icon to explore the 'record hints' to find out further possible leads for your ancestor among the collections on FamilySearch.

for you to listen to there and then; while some of the other learning experiences will provide the opportunity for studying, in between sessions, to help you gain hands-on experience, sometimes with marked coursework, and perhaps even a recognised professional academic qualification at the end.

From short online courses, to distance learning, whether simply for enjoyment, or to gain academic or professional qualifications, there are many genealogy-related courses to choose from. The prices range from c.£10 to in excess of £10,000. There truly is something for everyone. (Prices have not been stated as they are subject to change in the future. As you would expect a one hour talk would be at the lower end of the price bracket, while a 10-week course would command more, and an academic qualification would understandably command a premium price).

FAMILY HISTORY EVENTS

The organisations below run family history shows and conferences – usually providing a programme of talks, as well as exhibitor booths to visit. Some of the events are online, others in the real world, and a few are hybrid events – providing the opportunity for in-person and/or virtual attendance. As noted above, some provide post-event access to recordings of the presentations for a limited time, so do be sure to check this out – as you won't have time to attend all the talks live on the day.

RootsTech

- International three and a half day genealogy event.
- With keynote speakers, exhibition hall.
- In 2023 this will be held in Utah, with online attendance also possible.
- Classes in multiple languages.
- Focus on global genealogy search skills and sources.
- **www.rootstech.org/**

Family History Show

- One-day family history event from TheGenealogist & GenealogySupplies held near London and in York.
- With talks, exhibitor booths, and ask-the-expert opportunities.
- Online show with similar experiences also held annually.
- **https://thefamilyhistoryshow.com/**

The Really Useful Family History Show

- One-and-a-half day online events from the Family History Federation.
- With talks, exhibitor booths, and ask-the-expert opportunities.
- Recordings of presentations are made available for a limited time after the event.
- **www.familyhistoryfederation.com/events**

Back To Our Past Tickets

- Three-day event held in Dublin.
- With talks, exhibitor booths, and ask-the-expert opportunities.
- **https://backtoourpast.ie/**

Scottish Indexes Family History Conference

- An all-day online marathon of genealogy talks.
- Provided FREE by husband and wife team, Graham and Emma Maxwell.
- **www.scottishindexes.com/**

WHERE TO FIND OUT MORE EVENTS

There are numerous organisations holding genealogy events all around the globe. Once you get into genealogy the only thing you will wish for is that you have more hours in the day.

To find details of other courses, talks, conferences etc, see these publicity providers:

Conference Keeper

Listings of talks and conferences from libraries, websites and family history organisations from around the globe.

https://conferencekeeper.org/

GENEVA

A go-to site for genealogy event listings, with a UK focus.

http://geneva.weald.org.uk/

Diary Dates

The *Family History Workbook for Beginners* is from the publishers of *Family Tree. Family Tree* is a monthly magazine (available in print and digital editions) – and in every issue details of upcoming events and courses, are listed.

To buy the magazine, see **www.family-tree.co.uk**

FAMILY HISTORY LEARNING EXPERIENCES THAT INTEREST ME

Topic: ....

Date: ....

Price: ....

Web: ....

Location: ....

Topic: ....

Date: ....

Price: ....

Web: ....

Location: ....

Topic: ....

Date: ....

Price: ....

Web: ....

Location: ....

Topic: ....

Date: ....

Price: ....

Web: ....

Location: ....

Top archive websites

Explore archive websites to discover what's out there to help you

Many of today's modern archives offer vast digitised collections.

Below are key national archives from around the British Isles. Take time to:

- explore their online catalogues
- see what records they have available online (some free, some paid-for access)
- jot down the details of items you'd like to study when you visit the archives, or to download at a later date
- note down collections that are of particular interest to you

TIP!

There are thousands of local and specialised archives, and one of these may hold just the records you need for your research. Check out this link to find archives throughout the UK: http://discovery.nationalarchives.gov.uk/find-an-archive

10 minutes a day for 7 days

Select one of the websites below and set yourself a goal to spend 10 minutes a day for a week, exploring the guides, collections and search tips for that site. This know-how will stand you in good stead.

www.nrscotland.gov.uk/research/catalogues-and-indexes

Search catalogues and indexes for the National Records of Scotland, the National Register of Archives for Scotland and the Scottish Archive Network

☐ Yes I've explored the site

☐ And I've browsed the research guides **www.nrscotland.gov.uk/research/research-guides**

Notes of guides & collections of interest:

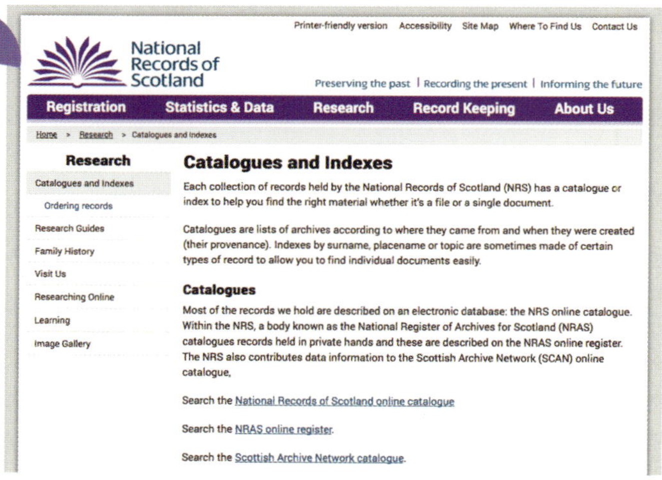

It's a great idea to keep a research log: this can include 'notes to self' about records you may like to explore in the future. Download the template Research Log from the Workbook web page: www.family-tree.co.uk/information/fhwfb

http://discovery.nationalarchives.gov.uk

Access 32 million catalogue descriptions, searching 2,500 archives across the UK or solely searching The National Archives' holdings. 9 million records are available as downloads (some paid, some free access)

☐ Yes I've explored the site

☐ And I've browsed the research guides **www.nationalarchives.gov.uk/help-with-your-research/research-guides-keywords/**

Notes of guides & collections of interest:

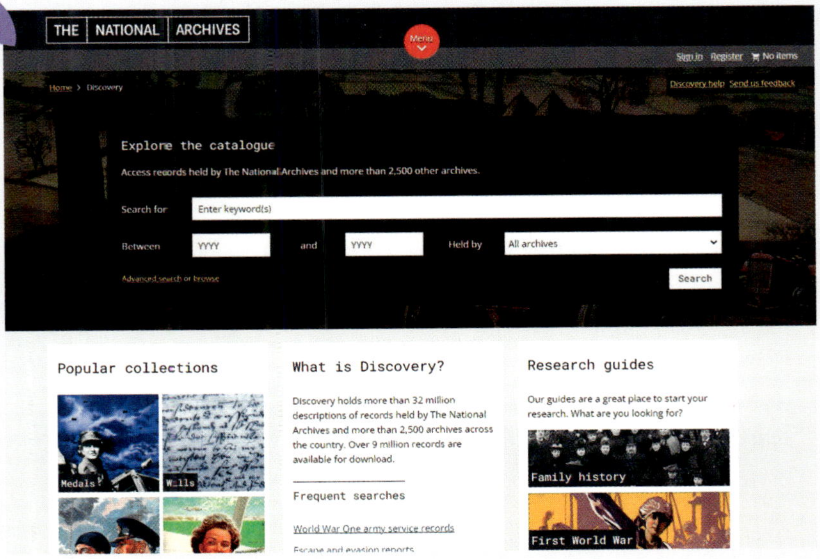

www.nls.uk

Explore digitised maps, directories, journals and images, free on the National Library of Scotland website

☐ Yes I've explored the site

☐ And I've browsed the digital resources and catalogues **www.nls.uk/digital-resources/** and **www.nls.uk/catalogues/**

Notes of guides & collections of interest:

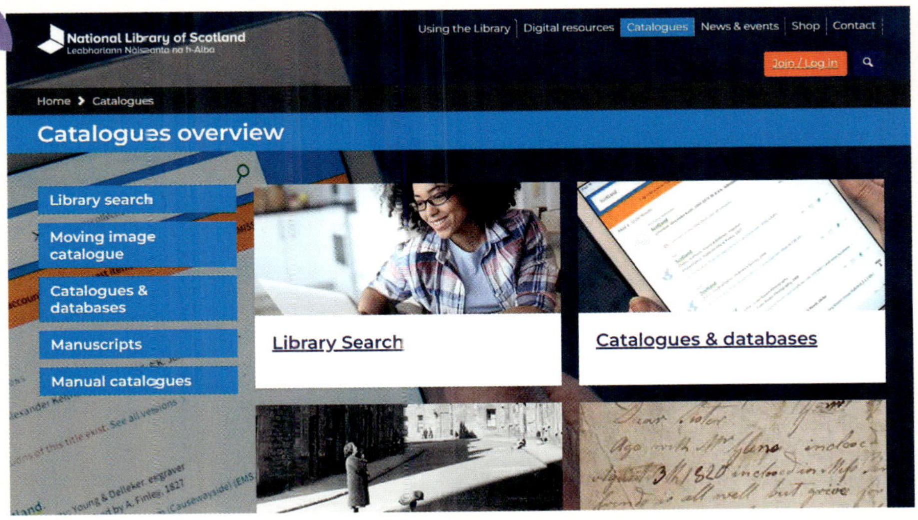

www.llgc.org.uk

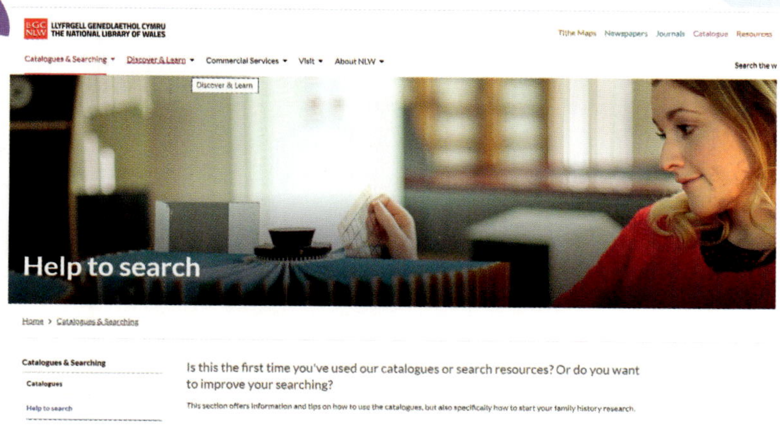

Search the online catalogue and the National Library of Wales extensive digital collections, including free access to over a million history newspaper pages, tithe maps and more

- ☑ Yes I've explored the site
- ☑ And I've browsed the help guides **www.library.wales/catalogues-searching/help-to-search/**

Notes of guides & collections of interest:

www.bl.uk/catalogues-and-collections/digital-collections

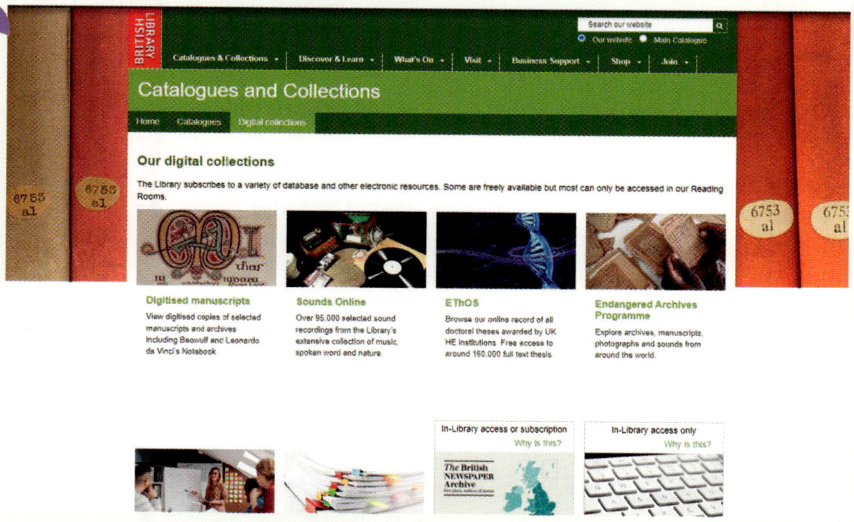

Investigate the 56 million items listed in the British Library's online catalogue

- ☑ Yes I've explored the site
- ☑ And I've browsed the Research Guides **www.bl.uk/catalogues-and-collections/digital-collections**

Notes of guides & collections of interest:

www.nationalarchives.ie/search-the-archives

Study the collections held at the National Archives of Ireland, including digitised collections such as census and wills too

☐ Yes I've explored the site

☐ And I've browsed the genealogy guides **www.nationalarchives.ie/genealogy/**

Notes of guides & collections of interest:

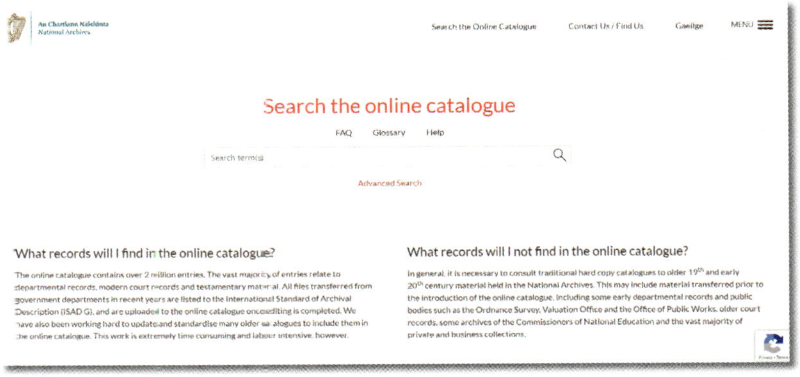

____

____

____

____

____

____

www.nidirect.gov.uk/proni

Explore the freely available digital facsimiles of original records in the Public Record Office of Northern Ireland

☐ Yes I've explored the site

☐ And I've browsed the resources and learning guides **www.nidirect.gov.uk/information-and-services/public-record-office-northern-ireland-proni/resources-and-learning**

Notes of guides & collections of interest:

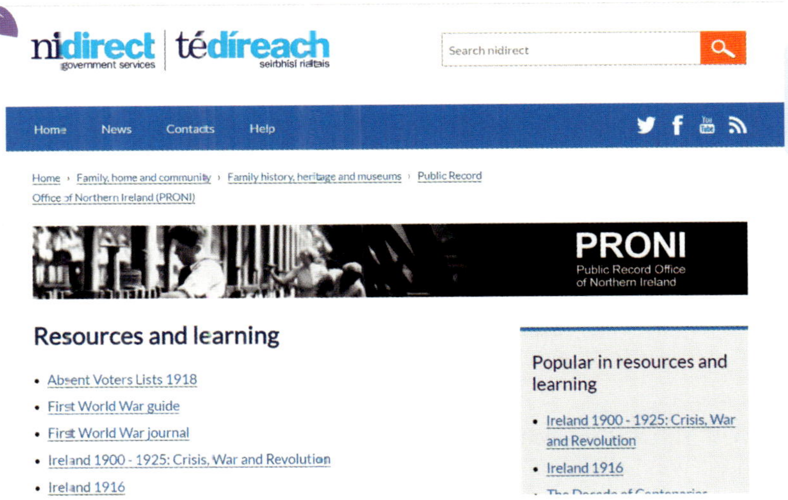

____

____

____

____

____

____

____

____

VISITING ARCHIVES

There are thousands of archives around the UK alone, let alone globally, and many of these have collections that span back a thousand years. So... if you love history, it's a massive shame not to make use of the historical treasures they hold. Our tips to follow will give you the know-how to take that step...

I have never visited an archive before, how can archives help me?

A Archives hold collections of records that will really enrich your understanding and appreciation of your family's history.

Typically you'll be searching for records to help you learn about your ancestors' lives and the places they once lived and worked.

From records about vital life events (baptisms etc), to occupational records, vestry minutes and poor law records, hospital and asylum records, manorial records, trade directories, maps and so much more, archives hold a vast variety of records that span many centuries.

While the key records (eg census and birth, marriage and death records) are helpfully available online, think of these as just the bare bones of your family tree. To really get an understanding of your ancestors' lives and times, it's well worth visiting the relevant archives.

Plus when you visit an archive you get the opportunity to (very carefully!) handle beautiful old contemporary documents created at the time of your ancestors' lives and hold history in your hands.

How can I prepare for my family history archive visit?

A To make the most of your trip to the archive you need to:

- make sure the records you wish to see will be available
- be sure to pack the notes and equipment you need
- & check the archive opening times and any pre-booking and identity requirements.

1. Checking the records are available

It's well worth ensuring that the records you want to study will be available.

Some records aren't held on site, so need to be pre-ordered. Pre-ordering is also helpful to make the most of your time in the archives, so that the ones you need are waiting for you when you arrive, and aren't in use by anyone else.

You can research the records you wish to view using the archives online catalogue. Where available, use the online booking form to place your pre-orders in advance of your visit.

2. Your notes

Be sure to pack your relevant notes, and a family tree chart, to help you.

If you keep a research log, you can use it to make a note of which records you need to search and which archives they are held at. Then you will be easily able to refer to your log and make a list of all the things you'd like to find out on your visit to the archives. You can additionally use the Archives Visit Check List.

TIP! For downloadable templates see **www.family-tree.co.uk/information/fhwfb**

3. Your tools for the day

Many archives let you take photos (perhaps for a small fee), and use your mobile phone, tablet, laptop etc in the search rooms. Be sure to charge your devices and set them to silent.

Remember to pack pencils (without erasers on the end) and loose leaf blank paper for taking notes (often notepads are not allowed).

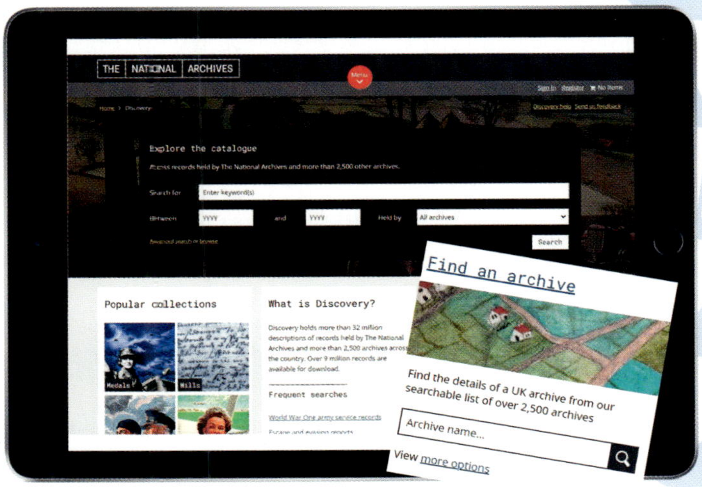

Scroll down the home page of the National Archives website to locate the 'Find an archive' facility. 'Find an archive' provides details for thousands of archives

4. Your ID

Lastly, remember to pack your archives ID so that you can access the search rooms. This may be your Archives Card, or, for instance your British Library Card or National Archives Reader's Ticket.

If you don't yet have the necessary card or ticket, check the website for the archive you wish to visit to find specific information about the identification paperwork you need to bring (eg typically passport, driving licence, household bill etc).

Can I order document copies from archives?

A Yes, certainly. Many archives offer document copying services. The usual process is to search the online catalogues, identify the records you want copies of, make a note of the archive references, and then email the archives to request a quote for the copying of the documents. The archives will then let you have the quote and you can decide whether to proceed. Ordering documents can be much more efficient than making a trip to the archives, if you're short of time or if the archive in question is located far from you.

How do I find which archives have online records or catalogues?

A If you know the archive's web address, any online catalogue they may have will be accessible from there. Alternatively you can search the 'Find an archive' map at **https://discovery.nationalarchives.gov.uk/find-an-archive** – and from here home in on archives for the area you're interested in, and click through to that archive's website.

The catalogues that are available online vary enormously, and the collections within them may be catalogued at a range of levels. In an ideal world all items would appear in the catalogue with full descriptions and name indexes. This would make it so quick and easy for us as family historians to find what we need.

However, constraints of resources mean that this is by no means always possible. Online catalogues are nevertheless extremely helpful for exploring which records an archive holds and, where possible, placing a pre-order on the document you wish to study when you make your archive visit.

Exploring archives from home

Remember to use your Family History Workbook for Beginners resources: they include useful forms for you to download and fill in. For instance, while you are researching your family history online at home you can gradually collate a list of the archives that you wish to visit, and the documents that you wish to view there. Download the Archives Visit Check List

Tip! Be sure to keep detailed notes including the archive references – then the archivists will be able to lay their hands on the records you want, and you won't waste time re-hunting for the details.

3 easy ways to find information

When doing family history there is a huge amount to learn, and to remember. Don't worry if you feel a little overwhelmed. Here are three extremely useful websites that will help you find the information you need. They are websites you are likely to wish to visit time and time again – treasure troves!

THE NATIONAL ARCHIVES RESEARCH GUIDES – STEP-BY-STEP

WHERE DO I GO TO FIND THE RESEARCH GUIDES?

Step 1: Go to **https://discovery.nationalarchives.gov.uk/** and click through to 'Browse All Research Guides' (over on the right-hand side of the screen).

1

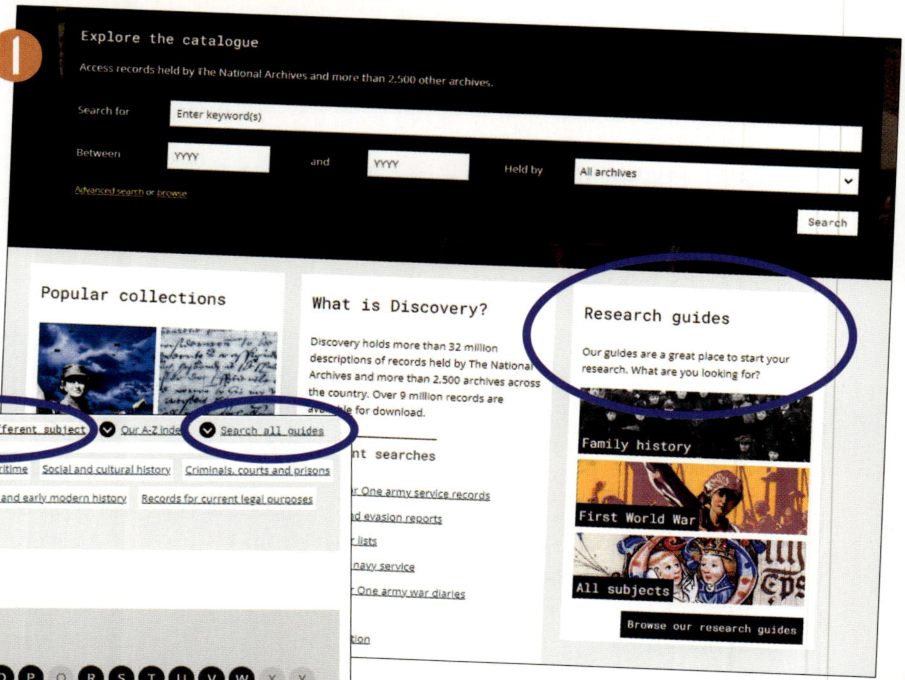

2

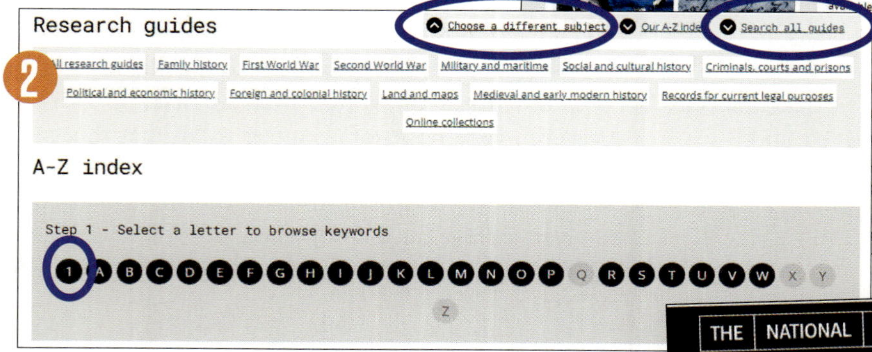

WHAT WILL I FIND?

Step 2: Here you can view the list A-Z. Selecting 'Choose a Different Subject' will bring up a list of categories, while selecting 'Search All Guides' will allow you to bring up a list of all the guides that are relevant to your search term.

There are more than 100 guides and they range from abbeys to wills. Selecting '1' at the start of the A-Z list will reveal guides concentrating on research in specific centuries, e.g. 1800s, 1700s etc.

3

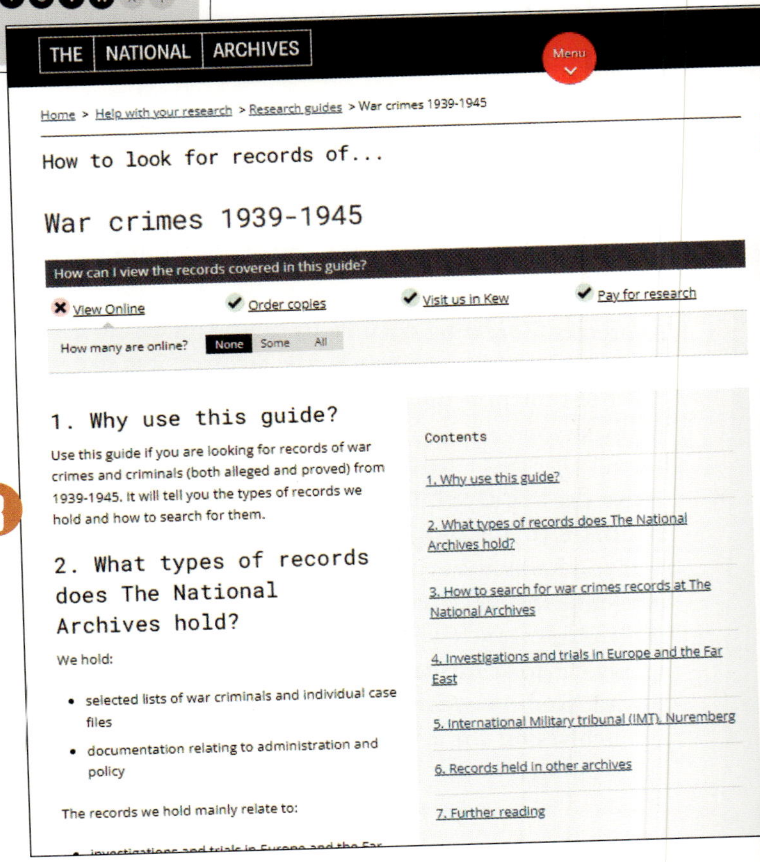

WHY WILL THEY HELP ME?

Step 3: The Research Guides are extremely useful, covering background information to the types of records relevant to the subject, as well as information about the specific record collections that will be of use to you, further reading ideas, and recommendations of other guides that may be useful to you. If the records have been digitised, for instance by a third party (e.g. available on another website, such as Ancestry, Findmypast or TheGenealogist) the Research Guide will provide a link.

Note: in such instances you are likely to be able to search the indexes on the third party websites but you will usually need a subscription (i.e. will need to pay to view the full details and to see the digitised copy of the original record).

The National Archives also has some digitised records available on its own website.

The National Archives Research Guides are not just for beginners – they are packed with useful information about the record collections you can enjoy searching while investigating your family history and you will likely find yourself referring to them for many years to come.

Tip! When visiting an archive website be sure to explore the range of guides they may have published about their collections. This will ensure you make best use of your time and don't miss out on archival treasures.

FAMILYSEARCH WIKIS – STEP-BY-STEP

WHERE DO I GO TO FIND THE WIKIS?

Step 1: Go to **https://www.familysearch.org/**. Select 'Search' from the menu, and scroll down to 'Research Wiki'.

1

WHAT WILL I FIND?

Step 2: Here you'll be presented with a map of the world, as the FamilySearch website helps people globally to research their family trees. There are currently more than 103,000 wiki articles to read. Some will relate to a specific place, others to a type of record. Use the wiki search bar to begin exploring your places and topics of interest.

2

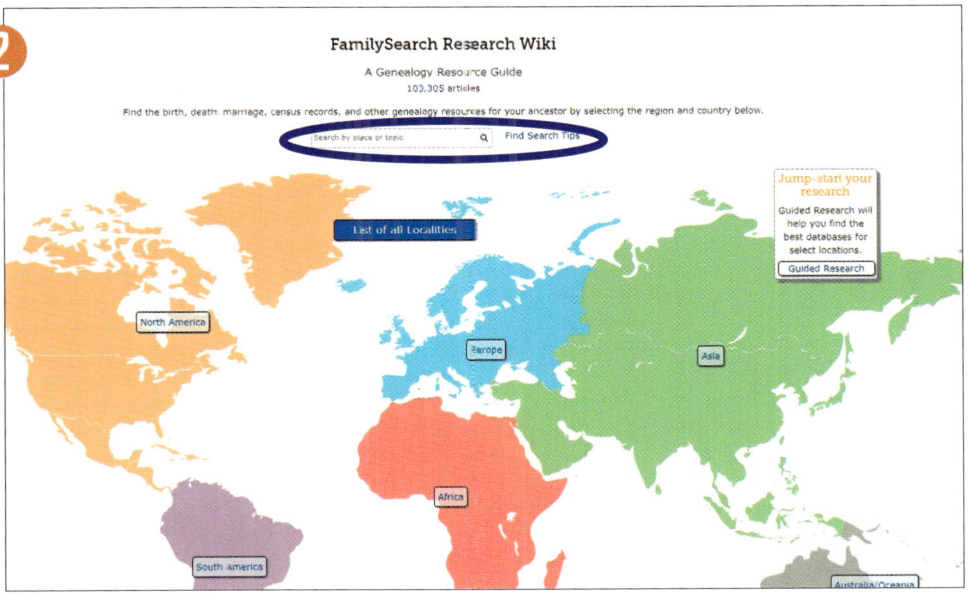

WHY WILL THE WIKIS HELP ME?

Step 3: The FamilySearch wikis provide a one-stop shop of information. On each wiki page you will find the key record collections listed, with links to research aids specific to that place included, and over on the right-hand side of each wiki page is a comprehensive list of further records to explore.

The beauty of the FamilySearch Wikis is that they are extremely detailed. For instance, they will specify a table showing exactly which years the baptism records for a single parish survive. It is this sort of precise information you need when doing family history.

Tip! If you can't find an ancestor in a place you would expect, then check: have the records survived? The FamilySearch Wiki will very likely be able to help you work out whether they have.

CYNDISLIST – STEP-BY-STEP

WHERE DO I GO TO FIND THE LIST?

Step 1: Go to **https://www.cyndislist.com/**.

1

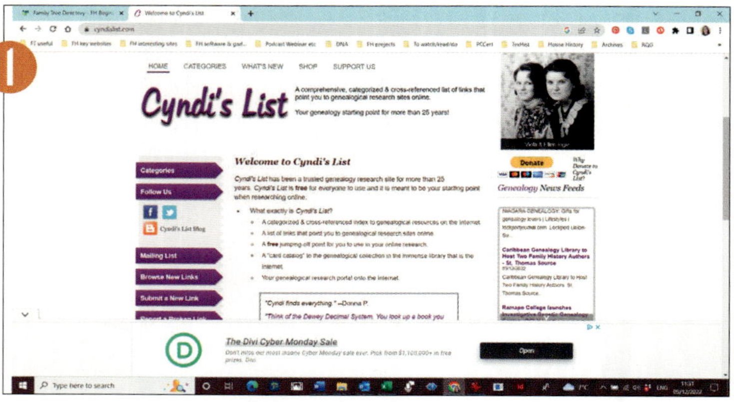

WHAT WILL I FIND?

Step 2: CyndisList is an online directory of more than 316,000 genealogy-related web links, sorted into 219 categories. Cyndi Ingles (the person behind CyndisList) has been growing her list for more than 25 years. Shown below are just some of the topics listed under 'S' – they are of worldwide interest, and extremely wide ranging.

Cyndi's List - Browse Categories Alphabetically - S

2

- Scandinavia & the Nordic Countries (70)
  Updated September 14, 2022
- Scanners & Scanning (55)
  Updated October 6, 2022
- Schools (490)
  Updated November 1, 2022
- Schwenkfelder (11)
  Updated January 4, 2021
- Scrapbooks (128)
  Updated May 27, 2022
- Search Engines (65)
  Updated November 7, 2022
- Serendipity in Genealogy (7)
  Updated August 1, 2019
- Servitude: Indentures, Serfs, Apprentices, etc. (99)
  Updated October 21, 2022
- Seventh-day Adventist (36)
  Updated May 13, 2017
- Shakers: United Society of Believers in the Second Coming of Christ (24)
  Updated August 5, 2022
- Ships & Passenger Lists (757)
  Updated November 1, 2022

3

Scandinavia & the Nordic Countries » Language, Names, Handwriting & Script

4 Links

- FamilySearch Learning Center - Scandinavian Handwriting
- FamilySearch Learning Center - Scandinavian Handwriting Part 3
- GramTrans
  GramTrans
- Nordic Names
  Comprehensive site on given names in Sweden, Denmark, Norway, Finland, Iceland, Greenland and the Faroe Islands.

WHY WILL IT HELP ME?

Step 3: Clicking through from a topic you'll be able to navigate specifically to the topic of interest to you. For instance, perhaps you'd like to learn about Scandinavian resources to help you learn the language and how to read the historic handwriting.

Tip! Browse CyndisList for inspiration as to the many routes down which you can take your family history research. She has links to cover all aspects of family history and from numerous countries too.

CLAIM YOUR FREE VIDEO COURSE

EXPERT VIDEO GUIDES TO HELP YOU WITH YOUR RESEARCH

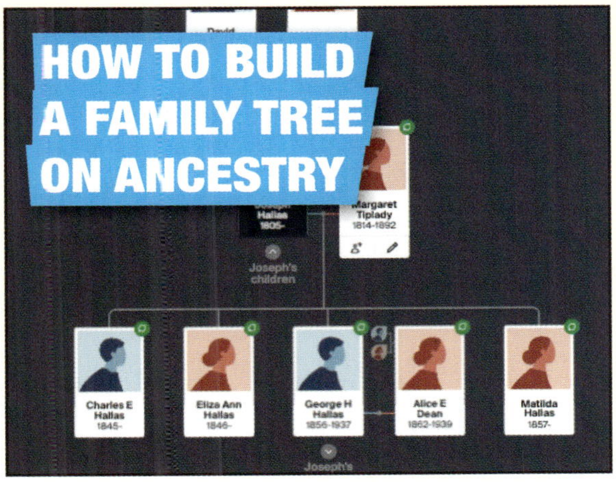

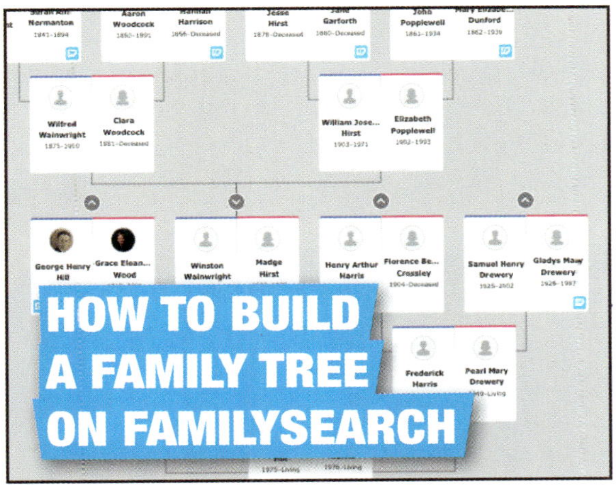

HOW TO CLAIM YOUR FREE VIDEOS:

Just visit the link below, sign up for the free *Family Tree* newsletter and you'll receive an exclusive link to view the videos. Plus, you'll receive friendly updates, tips, offers and more from the *Family Tree* team.

CLAIM YOUR FREE VIDEOS NOW AT:

WWW.FAMILY-TREE.CO.UK/ACCOUNT/REGISTER

STAYING ORGANISED

Keep your family history discoveries in the organised manner they deserve – you've worked hard to find them! We have advice to help you create tip-top files, well-preserved heirlooms and beautiful display charts

I'm suffering from information overload, how can I keep my family history research organised?

A It doesn't take long before the details you're gathering soon mount up, does it?

To keep track of all the fascinating information you're accruing, you need to set up a system to help you keep organised. These are the key elements that your system will need to include:

a) **A filing system for paper records** (these will include such things as inherited family papers, certificates, newspaper clippings). This system could include certificate folders (ring binders with pockets), for instance.

b) **An archiving system** for looking after heirloom photos and artefacts. This could include archive quality storage boxes, packaging and albums, to best preserve the items.

c) **A digital filing system** for logically storing all the digital documents that you will download from the web (eg census documents etc). For this you can set up folders and a file naming system on your computer. It's always best not to overcomplicate things, so you may initially just wish to create one folder called, eg, 'My family history'. Every document you add to the folder can then be given a name to help it be easy to find: perhaps have the surname first, then first name, a date, an indication of the document type.

Eg EASTWOOD_Susan_1891_birth_certificate

It's never too soon to get organised

Throughout the *Family History Workbook for Beginners* are lots of ideas for getting organised.

There is no right or wrong format – you will find the way that suits you best. It is likely that a combination of traditional paper-based filing systems, and digital filing options utilising your computer, tablet and mobile phone, will together provide you with the optimum help.

d) **A research recording system** This could be family history software capable of keeping notes and creating a family tree chart; or it could be a paper notebook, ring binder and printed family tree. You may wish to use both – paper and digital resources.

Why are these 4 points important?

Points a) and b), above, will help you look after and grow a family history archive of ancestor material for preserving for future generations. Points c) and d) will help you keep track of your research – making a note of what you've discovered, why you've deduced what you have, and most importantly recording who is related to who and how.

Make the system work for you

You may wish to use both – paper and digital resources, of course. The main thing, however, is that you create a system that suits the way you work. Starting with the most simple system possible will make you more likely to use it, and you can always fine-tune it as you go along.

The traditional filing system

The old-school paper way is to get a ring binder, with four dividers, one for each grandparent's line. To find out more, search online for the 'Mary Hill Colour Coding System' and you will find numerous guides and blogs by fans of the system.

See page 60 for tips on how to organise your paper family history folders.

Building your tree online

Many of the major data websites (Ancestry, FamilySearch, Findmypast, TheGenealogist (via TreeView) and MyHeritage) provide online family tree builders, to which you can add your information. Plus there are additional standalone online family tree builders, such as Famberry and TribalPages.

Page 32 has general points to consider about online tree-building. See page 36 for tips on how to organise your online family tree on Ancestry and page 40 for FamilySearch tips.

Choosing a family history program

You may also wish to collect your family history research on your computer. If so there are a number of family history programs in which you can:

- grow your family tree
- add research notes
- create a vast variety of research reports

- make customisable family tree charts
- add photos & documents
- analyse and filter your research
- set reminders & create to-do lists
- create a family history website
- & much, much more.

Is family history software suitable for you?

Yes. Such family history programs are suitable for people new to family history but, in addition, most of them are complex software capable of advanced research projects too. Just take it slow, master the basic functionality, and then dive deeper to learn about additonal tools that the software provides.

There are programs available for PC, Mac, Linux, and for use from the cloud too.

Some of the programs will allow you to search the major databases (often via a subscription) for further information to add to your research.

Some will allow you to sync your research – so that you can have it on your computer, and added to the cloud or an associated app too. This can be useful, enabling you to access your research via your smart phone while out and about.

Major current family history software programs include:

- Family Historian
- Family Tree Maker
- Legacy Family Tree
- RootsMagic
- TreeView
- Reunion (Mac)

Try out the trial & free versions

A number of the family history programs offer limited free versions; while they don't offer access to all the tools in the program, they can be used on a permanent basis very usefully. Other programs offer a time-limited free trial to the full version.

It's worth looking around and having a play with the various options out there before deciding which one to buy.

For cut-down free versions, see:

Legacy Family Tree Standard – **https://legacyfamilytree.com/downloadlegacy.asp**

RootsMagic Essentials – **https://www.rootsmagic.com/try/rootsmagic/**

TreeView Lite – **https://treeview.co.uk/download/** (this gives you 30 days' access to the full software; aftewhich it becomes TreeView Lite)

For a 30-day free trial version of Family Historian see – **https://www.family-historian.co.uk/downloads/free-30-day-trial**

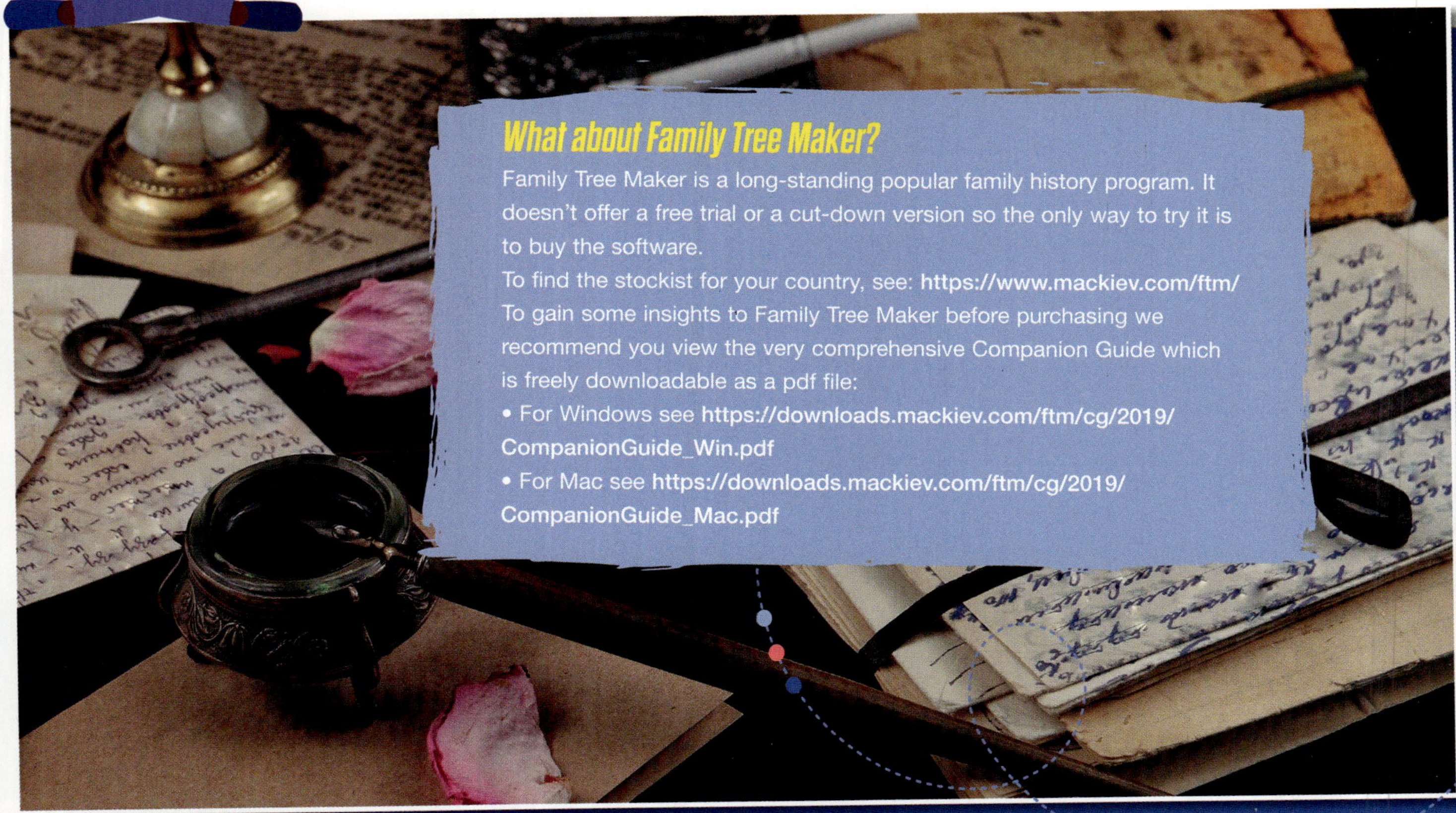

What about Family Tree Maker?

Family Tree Maker is a long-standing popular family history program. It doesn't offer a free trial or a cut-down version so the only way to try it is to buy the software.

To find the stockist for your country, see: **https://www.mackiev.com/ftm/**

To gain some insights to Family Tree Maker before purchasing we recommend you view the very comprehensive Companion Guide which is freely downloadable as a pdf file:

- For Windows see **https://downloads.mackiev.com/ftm/cg/2019/CompanionGuide_Win.pdf**
- For Mac see **https://downloads.mackiev.com/ftm/cg/2019/CompanionGuide_Mac.pdf**

Key questions to ask yourself when thinking about buying a family history program

Check list

Here is a check list of things to look out for, so that you can ensure the program you choose will serve you well for a long time:

• What sort of family tree chart displays and range of reports can the program create?
• Does it allow you to add notes, documents, photos, multimedia and sources?
• Does it have GEDcom import and export? This is important as it means, for instance, that you can share your research with fellow family members, and can more readily transfer your research to another program or website.
• Does it allow you to search your preferred subscription website from the software?
• Does it have a support group, Facebook group or up-to-date FAQ section etc (you want software that the software publishers are still actively supporting)?

I'd like to get a large paper family tree to display on my wall, what can you recommend?

A There are several options and things to consider. Will your family tree chart be a working document, to which you'll continue to add details as you find them? If so think about poster-style charts such as those from Twiggli and MyHistory for you to fill in by hand. Or is your chart the result of your research? In this case you could have it professionally printed, by, for instance, Genealogy Printers or Newtown Designs or MyHistory.

I love using my mobile for family history, can you recommend any good apps?

A Popular apps for family historians include:

• **Evernote** – to help you keep your research note-taking organised
• **Ancestry, Findmypast, MyHeritage, TreeView** and **FamilySearch** – for growing your online family tree
• **BillionGraves** – for adding and sharing photos of gravestones.

Don't forget the generic apps on your phone too: such as the voice recorder, spreadsheets, notes, reminders etc.

How to organise your family tree research

Through the Family History Workbook for Beginners you will have seen many mentions about the importance of keeping your research orderly. Now you may be wondering – "But how?". Here we will show you a simple way of keeping your findings organised by your four grandparents.

The system of organising your family tree research by your four grandparents is traditionally used for paper-based folders. However it does translate to digital records very well. In this instance, we will just be referring to paper-based folders for simplicity.

Step 1: Buy 4 ring binders – one for each of your 4 grandparents.

The traditional convention is to opt for the primary colours of red, blue and yellow, plus green.

This has the added advantage that you will readily be able to buy file dividers, stickers, and other stationery items that colour-match.

Step 2: Allocate each grandparent a colour.

Mary E.V. Hill is the genealogist accredited with coming up with the colour-coding by grandparent system, and she used blue and green for father's side, and red and yellow for mother's side, thus:

- Blue – for paternal grandfather.
- Green – for paternal grandmother.
- Red – for maternal grandfather.
- Yellow – for maternal grandmother.

The main thing is that you always use the same colour for the same grandparental line across all your filing (eg if you choose blue for your paternal grandfather then also use blue for any other folders that you create for him and his ancestors). This will help ensure that you can see at a glance which branch of the family you're working on (particularly useful, for instance, if you have Jones, or Smiths, on a few branches of your tree).

Step 3: Gather & sort!

Collect up all the family history information you have come across so far, and sort it into the four grandparental branches of your family tree. You should have 4 piles (or boxes if you wish) in front of you.

Choose your paternal grandfather's branch, and sort the material into his father's and mother's sides. If needed repeat the process.

File up the material, using dividers with ancestor names on. It can feel confusing as your family tree will consist of couples – so where and how do you store the material that relates to more than one person? There is no perfect answer and you need to develop a system for yourself. These are some things you will find helpful however:

1. Women are *always* filed under their maiden name, rather than their married name.
2. You may like to write surnames in UPPER CASE so that they are easy to spot.
3. Pedigree charts (aka family trees) usually place the male's name on the left-hand side of the couple, and the female's name on the right-hand side. You may like to order your folders this way too: starting with the father's father's line, and working over to the mother's mother's side, so that there is a consistent logic across your filing system.
4. Use family record sheets to provide summaries of the key details of each family group. Download the template Family Record Sheet from **www.family-tree.co.uk/information/fhwfb**.
5. You will find documents that refer to several family members, such as census records and marriage certificates. It may sound patriarchal to today's ears, but it can help to store the copy of the record under the groom's name (for

This is a pedigree chart showing the root person of the family tree, their parents, grandparents and great-grandparents.

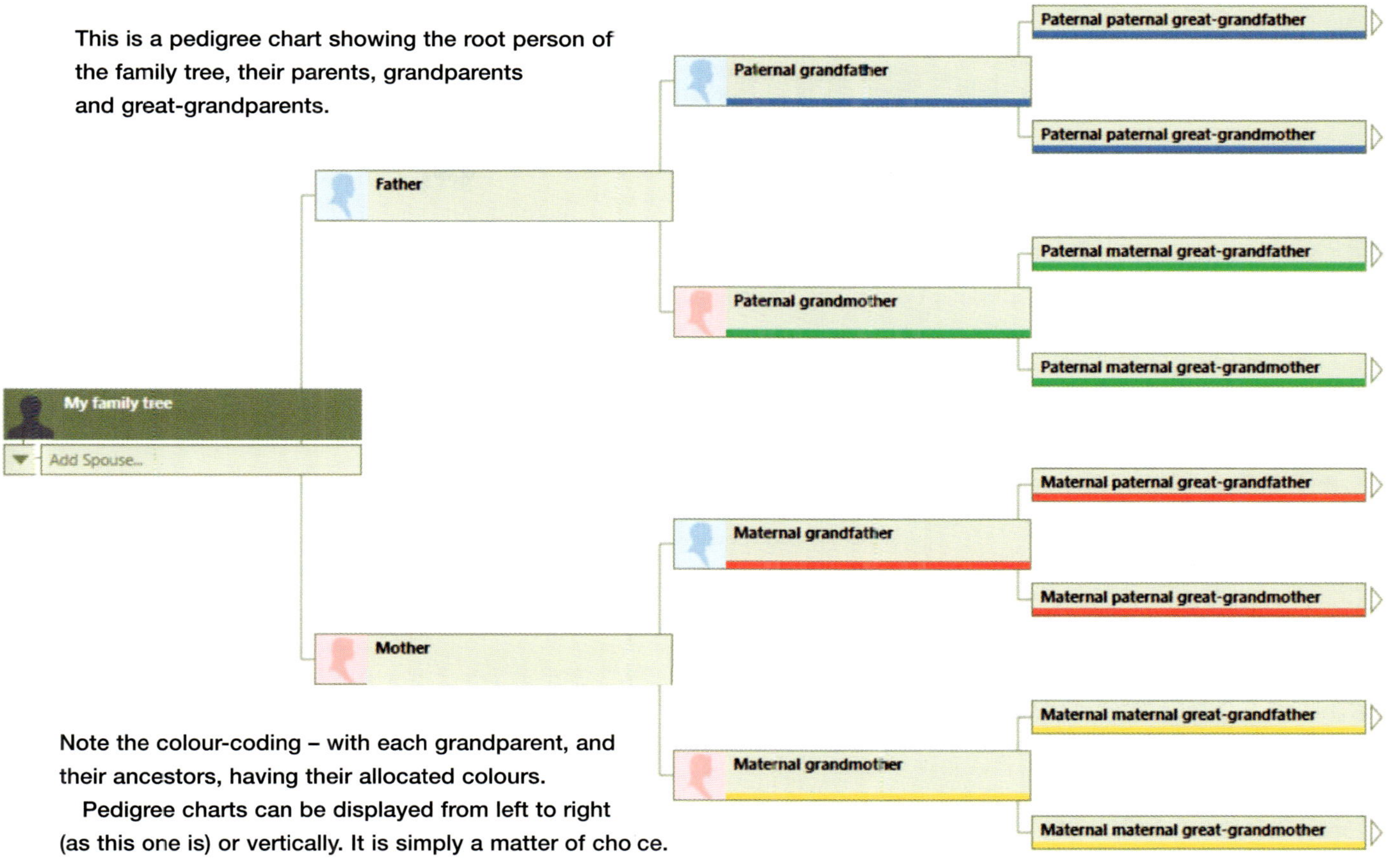

Note the colour-coding – with each grandparent, and their ancestors, having their allocated colours.

Pedigree charts can be displayed from left to right (as this one is) or vertically. It is simply a matter of choice.

a marriage certificate) and under the name of the head of the household (for a census). Under the bride's name you can enter a cross-reference, reminding yourself to view the marriage certificate under the groom's name. If you decide to place a copy of a record under each name this could soon become extremely bulky, but it is up to you, your preferences and your available storage space. Whatever system you use you need to be able to apply it as consistently as you can across your records.

Why to grandparent level, rather than great-grandparent level?

This is a good question – why do we advise dividing your family tree filing system into just the four grandparents?

The answer is that you want to aim to keep your filing system as simple as possible. A simple system is one that you are far more likely to stick with. You can always finetune it and make it more specific as you go.

Remember that with family history, with each generation you trace back in time the number of direct ancestors you have doubles: 4 grandparents, 8 great-grandparents, 16 great-great-grandparents, 32 great-great-great-grandparents.

While we do hope that you will soon find yourself tracing your great-great-great-grandparents, maybe 32 ring binders is a little too many to store on your bookshelves … just yet.

On a more serious note, restricting your system will help you to keep it streamlined. It will be quite natural for you to find more information about some lines than others (for some lines you may find very little (even nothing), so you don't want to have empty folders languising.

Those precious originals

TIP! If you have original documents (such as birth certificates that have been handed down in the family you will want to treat these carefully).

Firstly – never hole punch, staple, paper clip or laminate original documents as these will damage them.

Secondly – consider buying archival quality filing wallets, suitable for binders, to preserve the paper and ink into the future. (For supplies see **www.my-history.co.uk** or **www.genealogysupplies.co.uk**).

Thirdly – consider just keeping a copy in your filing system, and store the original in your home archive (yes you can create your own home archive for storing original documents and old photographs in optimum conditions for preservation – see page 66).

Do you have to use the colour-coded filing system?

Not at all. Many people just find colour-coding a helpful visual aid.

TIP! Look out for the colour-coding tool on your family history software. Several programs offer colour-coding, such as Family Tree Maker, Family Historian, Legacy Family Tree and RootsMagic. If so, you can employ it and match the colours to your paper-based system.

YOUR PAPER FILING SYSTEM

We mentioned pedigree charts and family record sheets on the previous page. Below are an example of each.

- These two forms are of central use to a paper-based family history filing system.
- Even if you plan on storing your family history research largely online, they can be very handy forms to use while you are working on a particular ancestor and their family group – to conveniently note your findings, your suppositions etc, before committing them to your main online tree.
- To download the Pedigree Chart and Family Record Sheet templates, visit **www.family-tree.co.uk/information/fhwfb**. You may print and use as many copies as you wish for your personal files.

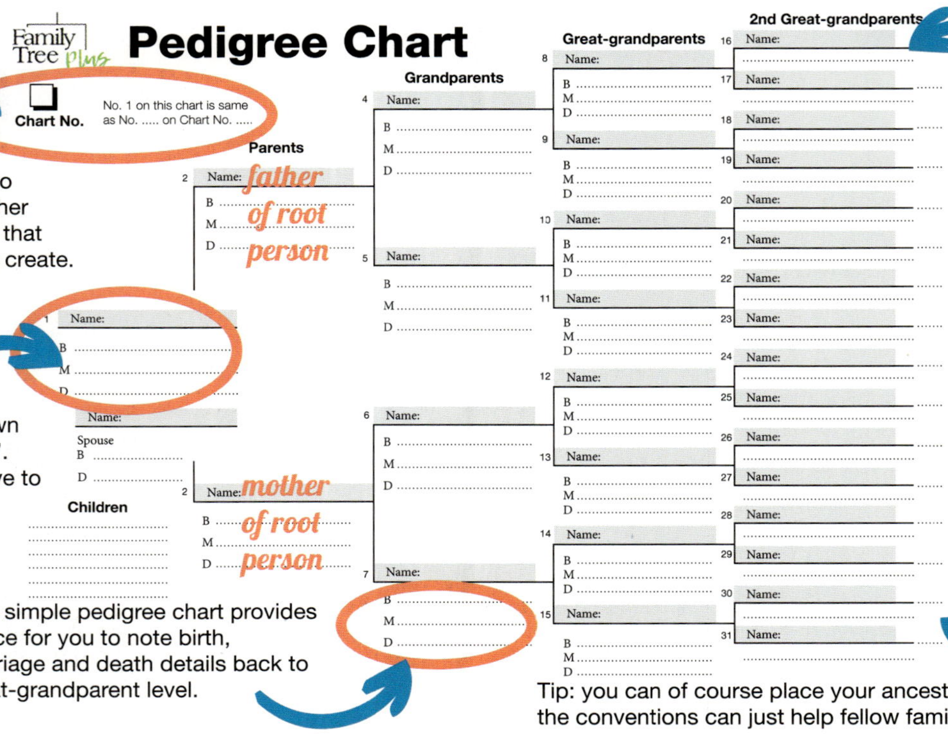

Note the ability to cross-refer to other Pedigree Charts that you may wish to create.

This person is known as the 'root person'. Note: it doesn't have to be you!

It is traditional to place the father's father's line of the root person at the top of a pedigree chart (or on the extreme left, if your pedigree chart is orientated vertically).

It is traditional to place the mother's mother's line of the root person at the bottom of the pedigree chart

This simple pedigree chart provides space for you to note birth, marriage and death details back to great-grandparent level.

Tip: you can of course place your ancestral lines differently; the conventions can just help fellow family historians to understand your workings

This simple Family Record Sheet packs a punch providing space for quite a bit of detail about an ancestral couple

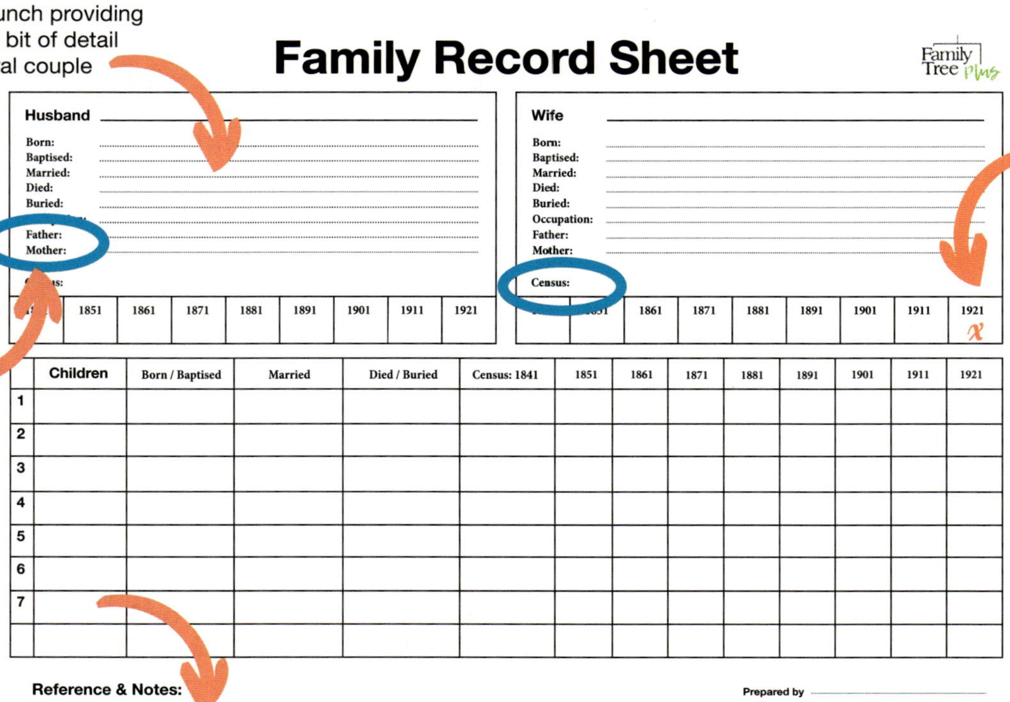

Here you can include the father and mother of the ancestral couple

Only occasionally will we find an ancestor born before the 1841 Census and still going strong in 1921. Once you have found the birth and death dates for your ancestor put a line through the census boxes that won't be relevant for them.

If your ancestral couple had more than 7 children, then create another Family Record Sheet and include a note to yourself in the notes section

Note: This form gives space for the census as it is such an important record for family history in the past few centuries. You can create your own Family Record Sheets more suitable to other eras and other nationalities for which the census 1841-1921 is not applicable. We hope you see how useful such an at-a-glance form may be to your records.

HOW TO ORGANISE YOUR DIGITAL FILES & FOLDERS

Learn a few simple steps to keep your digital family history files organised, right from the start.

There are billions of historic records that have been digitised and made available online. Some of these will be related to your ancestors. Exciting, isn't it! Before you know it, you can have a mass of documents saved to your computer… but, unless you decide to be organised, you can have little idea what each file is, without opening and studying it. Worse still you may have found a document, and can't remember where you've saved it on your computer. How frustrating would that be!?

To prevent yourself getting in this pickle, we have a set of steps, to help you keep your digital files organised right from the start. They provide a simple arrangement that you can expand as your research continues over the years.

ARRANGING YOUR DIGITAL FAMILY HISTORY FOLDERS

STEP 1:
Set up a folder on your computer called MY FAMILY HISTORY.

STEP 2:
Within your MY FAMILY HISTORY folder you are going to create several further folders:

DOCUMENTS
PHOTOS
AUDIO & VIDEOS

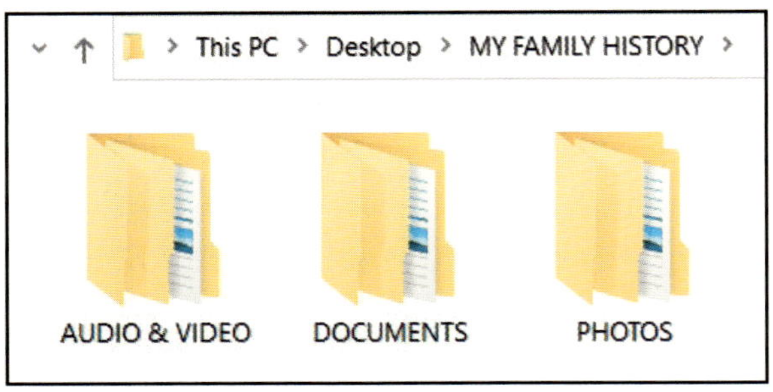

STEP 3:
Within *each* of the folders above (i.e. DOCUMENTS, PHOTOS, AUDIO & VIDEOS) you are going to create a further folder called POSSIBLES. It is in the POSSIBLES folders that you can file everything you are uncertain of – then you have your puzzles and possibles clearly stored, and know that you need to investigate them further.

THOUGHTS ON YOUR FOLDER HIERARCHY

Some people may like to create a folder for each grandparental branch of the family tree. If you wish to do so at this stage, that's fine. We would recommend that you use the same system across all your DOCUMENTS, PHOTOS, AUDIO & VIDEOS folders (i.e have a 'SMITH' folder in documents, in photos and in audio & videos).

You can name each grandparent folder by the full name or simply the surname of that grandparent.

At this stage, however, we are not going to implement these sub-folders for each grandparental branch. Your computer provides you with extensive sort and search capabilities, so we feel it is simpler to keep all your documents in a single folder called DOCUMENTS, and all the photos in PHOTOS etc.

NAMING YOUR FAMILY HISTORY FILES

Now we're going to look at how to name your family history files. To follow are recommendations that will help you see at a glance who each file relates to, what each file is about, and where you found the information. This is how we recommend naming your family history files.

Either by record type or by surname primarily. For instance:

Record type. SURNAME, first name. Date. Place. Website code/Collection.

or

SURNAME, first name. Date. Place. Record type. Website code/Collection.

Here are three examples.

First let's look at how you might name a file containing a copy of a page from the census, by record type:

Census 1871 Southampton EASTWOOD James Ancestry

And by surname:

EASTWOOD James 1871 Southampton Census Ancestry

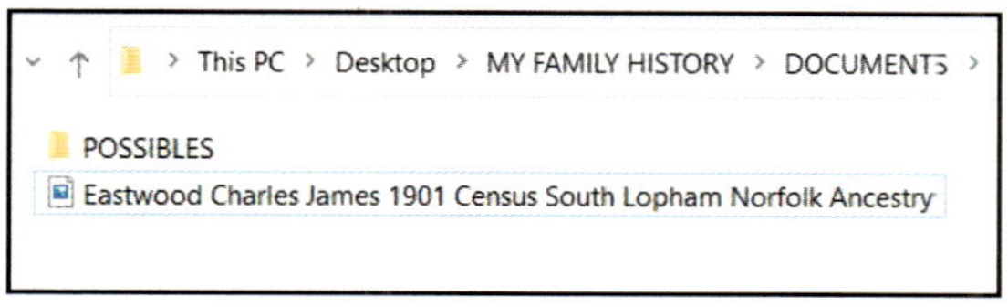

Next, let's look at how you might name a file containing a copy of a family photograph, by record type:

Photo Collection George HILL EASTWOOD James 1897 Brighton

And by surname

EASTWOOD James 1897 Brighton Photo Collection George HILL

These are simple file naming systems that have the

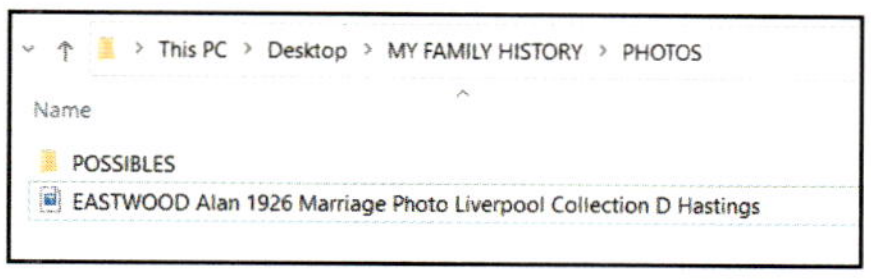

following advantages:

1. Your computer will be able to sort them into name, then date order.
2. You will be able to see at a glance what sort of item it is.
3. You will be able to see where you found the record online, or who holds the original (in the case of a family photo for instance, where we have included 'Photo collection George Hill' in the file name).

The system isn't perfect however, and does have some disadvantages. Such is the nature of family history filing systems. Let's reconsider that census file name above:

EASTWOOD James 1871 Southampton Census Ancestry

It is highly likely that there are other people named on the census page that belong in your family tree. Perhaps James Eastwood's wife and children, say. However it would make the file name unmanageably long if you were to include all their names. So, you will need to compromise. As with paper-based filing systems the main thing is to set up a system that you employ consistently across your family history files.

By always using the name of the head of the household for your census files, for instance, you will know that that is what you have done, and hence under whose name to look for the relevant document.

In addition, by adding the copies of the documents to your online family tree and/or your family history software on your computer, you will be able to tag the other relations that appear, for instance on the census page, or in the old group family photo, etc.

The way in which you arrange your digital family history files is entirely up to you. If you're an organised sort of person and already have a filing system for your digital files, that is good news, as we cannot encourage you enough to keep your family history files organised from the start. You will also find that whatever system you choose, you will evolve it – or even overhaul it completely – as time goes by. But, in the meantime, do get into the habit of naming your files clearly so that you can readily find them when you need them.

TIP!

Back up your family history files! Family history is very absorbing and you will likely spend many hours, days, weeks, months, ... years – tracing records about your ancestors. Be sure to make regular copies of your files and save them on an external drive (e.g. on a memory stick and/or – preferably 'and' as two copies are better than one – using a cloud-based service, such as Dropbox or GoogleDrive).

How to organise your HOME ARCHIVE & LIBRARY

Even if your goal is to be a digital-based family historian you will inevitably, hopefully, end up the curator of some of the family treasures, and are highly likely to gradually grow a nice (little or large) collection of family history books. Here we're going to look at curating, preserving and enjoying your family home archive and library.

YOUR HOME ARCHIVE

What might your home archive contain? This will depend vastly on what has been passed down from previous generations, who has inherited it, and whether you are in touch with them. For instance your second cousin may have a fabulous photo of your great-grandpa on the deck of a steamer bound for America… but would you know that? If you are fortunate, your home archive could, potentially, contain:

- Old photos
- Letters
- Newspaper clippings
- School reports
- Certificates
- Scrapbooks
- Recipe books
- Medals
- Deeds
- Inventories
- Samplers
- Items of clothing
- Memorabilia: items from sporting achievements, or holidays, for instance.

Clearly some of these two-dimensional items are easily stored in folders, in archive quality wallets. Other larger and bulkier items would need their own storage box. And some items you may like to have on display.

HOW BEST TO STORE

You may wish to have a selection of your family items on show for you, and others, to enjoy. This is of course a lovely idea, and to ensure they can be enjoyed for as many generations into the future as possible, be sure to keep items out of direct sunlight, which can have a bleaching and deteriorating effect.

If storing, choose a dry location that has a stable temperature: ideally in one of the rooms you use regularly in your home (not in an attic, basement or garage). If possible use archive quality storage products that will slow the deterioration of your photos and papers. They can be expensive, so you could gradually buy such storage items over time.

HOW TO ORGANISE OLD PHOTOS

The originals of old photographs are of course the crème de la crème of a family photo collection. However, it is extremely well worth taking the trouble to make *copies* of the originals. You can do so by scanning or making photographic copies of them. Once copied, be sure to save these copies in a safe place – such as on a drive that you keep at a relative's home or store them in the cloud. Then, should fire, flood or theft deprive you of the originals you will at least have the copies.

Download the 'Your Home Archive Catalogue' template from the Family History for Beginners Workbook resources web page.

HOW TO ORGANISE YOUR MEMORABILIA & HEIRLOOMS

Memorabilia and heirlooms are the sorts of items that may well interest the other members of the family a little more than the letters and photos, so it could be that other relations are the custodians of some of the family memorabilia and heirlooms.

If such items are in your possession you may wish to offer such items to your family members, as it may be difficult for you to find the space for everything.

SAVE THE STORIES

As the family's family historian you will understand that the value of the items as regards your ancestors' lives is in the *stories* that goes with the items – as that's what makes them precious to your family history.

So find a way to record these stories:

- You could simply type the story up and add it as a file to your family history software, or on a sheet of paper, filed with the relevant ancestor in your ring-binder.
- If the owner of the memorabilia or heirloom agrees you could take a photograph of the item and add that to your family history records.
- You could interview the person who heard the story about the item first-hand from the ancestor, and save it as an audio or video clip.

The importance of the stories can't be underestimated for what they add to your family history, and for how much more precious they make the item itself. For instance, without the story, the item may just look like 'an old ship in a bottle'; with the story, however, you will know that it was given to your mother, aged 6, by her father when he returned from serving in the Atlantic during the Second World War, and it was the first present he'd been able to give her for three years. (You get the idea, the story that goes with that old item really makes it special!).

CATALOGUE YOUR COLLECTION

What does this mean? At its simplest it just means: create a list of all the items in your family history collection. What should you include on the list? As much information as you can so that you and your family members know which ancestor the item came from and why it's important to your family history.

Include:

1. A description of the item.
2. Where is came from (original owner, previous owners(s).
3. Where it is now stored (where in your home, or with which other relation).
4. Whether you have a photo of the item (you could include this on your list, inserting the photo into a Word document or Excel sheet for instance).
5. The story that goes with the item (or a link to a blog of the story).

YOUR HOME LIBRARY

This sounds very grand doesn't it! There is something about 'family history' and 'books' that make them perfect partners, so you may find yourself getting quite a little collection of tomes over the years. Most of these are likely to be new publications, but you may wish to add vintage volumes to your home library. For instance, perhaps there is a trade publication that mentioned your ancestor, or maybe you just love the look of a Victorian edition of Mrs Beeton's cookery book.

Old, or new, paper-based or digital (e-books), we recommend that you write a list of all your family history books, and place it in the cloud or save it as a file on your mobile phone. Then, when you are out and about, and find a book of interest, you can quickly check whether you have it already!

For other advice on how to organise your family history see pages 60-62 for advice on a paper-based filing system, and pages 64-65 for advice on ordering and naming your digital documents and photos.

How do I start writing my family history?

This is such good news that you are interested in this question. After all, what a waste of your hard work researching and gathering the family history, if you are not going to share it now and in the future. Here are some steps to help you start writing that family story. This is one of the most important things you will undertake when doing your family history.

Writing your family history takes several stages. The first of which is to research and write notes about your ancestors' lives. If you've been following the tips woven through the *Family History Workbook for Beginners* you will already be well on the way with this, and will be keeping written notes about your family history discoveries (typed or handwritten is fine).

Tip! Check the pages on creating an online family tree using Ancestry (page 36) and/or FamilySearch (page 40). In there you will find where to start crafting a life story for each of your ancestors when building your online family trees.

Mind maps

Mind maps are really useful for gathering your thoughts and brainstorming topics you'd like to write about.

Use mind maps throughout your writing journey. For instance, you can create an initial mind map to help you decide on the subject of your book, topics you'd like to include etc. Or you can use a mind map to concentrate your focus on an individual ancestor, or choose to use a mind map for each chapter of your book to help you gather your thoughts.

We have created some mind map templates to get you started. Feel free to create your own, adding further 'thought bubbles' as your ideas grow.

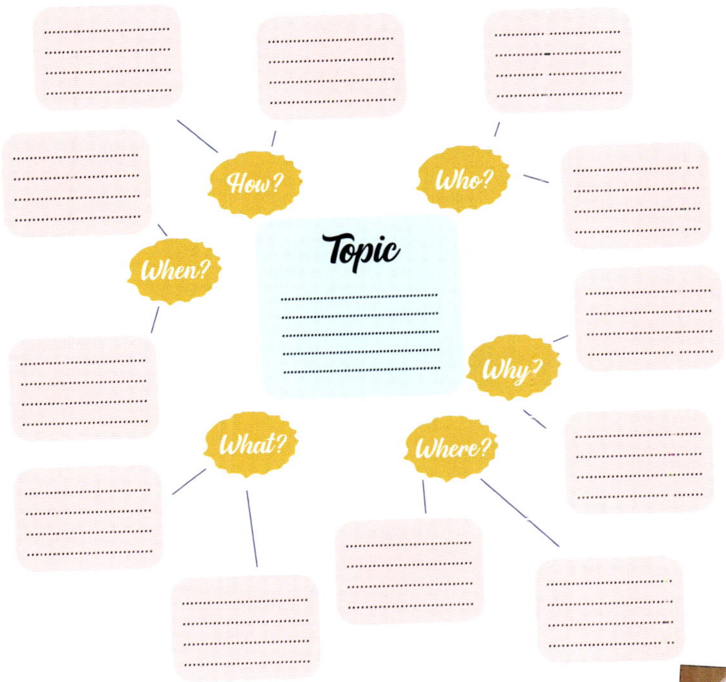

Deciding on the focus of your family story

The next steps is to plan your writing – to define what the focus of your story will be.

Are you planning on covering your entire family tree, or just a specific branch of your family, or people from a certain location, or perhaps an ancestral couple and their descendants?

Alternatively, perhaps you'd like to focus on a theme, concentrating on military ancestors, ancestors who travelled, or who all worked down the mine, ancestors' childhoods, or family recipes. Deciding on a focus will help you plan.

A mind-map can be a very useful way to start gathering your thoughts. Try out this example mind-map (see left). You can also download a printable version from the *Family History Workbook for Beginners* web link.

Planning your content (breaking it down further; what do you have; what do you need?)

Once you have your focus, you need to work out what material you already have, and what it is that you still need to find out. (Don't worry – when people come to "put pen to paper" that's when they realise that there are probably gaps that need to be filled in the family story).

In addition to words, you will need to be thinking about images too. You may be fortunate enough to have a collection of relevant family photos, if not you will need to think outside the box.

Once you have decided on your main focus, you will need to break it down into manageable chunks.

Use the planning sheet to write a summary of what you wish to cover in each chapter, noting possible images you'd like to include, and most importantly – a deadline by which you're going to get it done. Of course you don't need to set a deadline, but if writing your family history is something that you're really keen to see accomplished, then a deadline may help you do so!

Try out this example planning sheet (see right). You can also download a printable version from the *Family History Workbook for Beginners* web link: **www.family-tree.co.uk/information/fhwfb**.

Planning sheets

Chapter summary

(briefly, what you're going to cover)..

....

....

....

....

....

....

Illustration ideas

(notes on the photos, documents, maps, memorabilia etc that might provide suitable images)

....

....

....

....

....

Word count?

Your family history is unique to your family and how you write it is up to you.
You can write as much or as little as you wish, or as often as you wish.
Or you may like to set yourself a word count challenge, with a deadline, to help you reach your writing goal

I'll have my first 100 words completed by..

I'll have my first 500 words completed by..

I'll have my first 1,000 words completed by ....

Deadline for completion of:

I'll have my first draft of this chapter completed by:

....

I'll have the finished chapter completed by:

....

Your 'Publishing Your Family History' check list

- **Cover:**
If possible a photo or photo montage from your own collection would best fit your personal family history ☐

- **Title:**
If marketing your book online a clear 'what is says on the tin' title may help it be found by future readers ☐

- **Sub-title:** Useful to expand on your topic ☐

- **Blurb:**
A succinct summary to go on the outside back cover. Include testimonials here too if you wish ☐

- **Contents**:
This could include chapter headings. You may wish to write a few explanatory words about each ☐

- **Index:**
Include mentions for each of your ancestors, surnames, placenames and key events in your index ☐

- **Caption & image credits:**
A picture is much more interesting when you know what it depicts. Be sure to caption your images. Also include image credit lines, specifying 'image courtesy of X' or 'image © of X' etc ☐

- **Copyright:**
Include a note to express that the work is your copyright ☐

- **ISBN:**

If self-publishing and you would like an ISBN, it can be bought from **www.nielsenisbnstore.com/Home/Isbn/** Cost = £91 approx for one (or £169 for a block of 10 ISBNs). Note that paperback, hardback and ebooks each need their own ISBN, so a block is worth it. Free ISBNs are available to those self-publishing/publishing via Amazon; Amazon ISBNs only valid on Amazon platform ☐

- **Printer:**

Include the details of the printer's company name ☐

- **Blog & social media handles:**

Set up a blog to publicise your book. Free blogs can be set up at WordPress for instance. You may wish to set up social media handles for your publication too, or just tweet, Facebook and Instagram your publicity from your own account ☐

- **Thanks:**

If you wish, include a dedication to the family members who've supported or inspired you, or archivists or experts who have helped you write your book, etc ☐

Don't panic! If the thought of a book sounds daunting, don't worry. Of course the format in which you write your family history has so many possibilities. You may like to record your family history as a series of Word documents just for sharing with family, you may like to use PowerPoint to tell it as a slide show, or you may like to grab you mobile phone and record your favourite anecdotes there and then. These are all worthy endeavours for which the generations to come will thank you.

Your birth, marriage & death FINDING AID

The BMDs self-help guide is designed to help you begin finding the records and resources you need to look at next, in order to learn more about your ancestors' births, baptisms, marriages, deaths and burials

How does the family history self-help guide work?

The self-help guide includes some of the sorts of questions that we all ask ourselves in order to find the information we need. The aim of this self-help guide is to provide a few pointers to help people dive in and start making progress right away on finding the birth, baptism, marriage, death or burial details they seek.

Why do we mention birth, baptism, marriage, death and burial records?

The reason is due to how the records have developed over the centuries. From 1538 Thomas Cromwell stipulated that each parish in England and Wales must keep records of the baptisms, marriages and burials of its parishioners. These were the most comprehensive records of our ancestors for several centuries. Then, in 1837, the civil registers of births, marriages and deaths were introduced in England and Wales. For other countries the dates vary, as you'll see, but these 5 record types remain important.

Where should you look?

In family history, the question 'How do I…' is often first answered by 'It all depends…'. The answer you need will depend on the era and the geographical and topical area in which you're researching. As you will have seen, in the example just given (of civil registration records for England and Wales dating from 1837 onwards), different record collections span different date periods and locations.

What places does the self-help guide cover?

Largely the leads cover Britain and Ireland, but there is some information included for Australia, New Zealand, Canada and America.

What about if my ancestors come from somewhere else?

Try the FamilySearch Wiki:
www.familysearch.org/en/wiki/
(See page 53 of the Workbook)

Q I'd like to find my ancestor recorded in the civil registration birth/marriage/death indexes, what can I do?

My ancestor was born/married/died in:

England/Wales

From 1 July 1837 onwards: see **www.gro.gov.uk/gro/content/certificates/login.asp** (indexes to births 1837-1934 and 1984 onwards and deaths 1837-1957 and 1984 onwards, and from here you can order certificates).

See also **www.freebmd.org.uk** for indexes to births 1837-1989, marriages 1837-1990 and deaths 1837-1986. FreeBMD also has partial coverage, after these end dates, as the project is a work in progress. Use the index info to order certificates at the Gro.gov.uk link above.

On 30 June 1837 or earlier: see the parish registers question overleaf

Scotland

From 1 January 1855 onwards: **http://familytr.ee/scotbmd** (indexes to births, marriages and deaths from 1855). Plus you can see digitised copies of the full registers for births up to 100 years ago, marriages up to 75 years ago and deaths up to 50 years ago. Copy certificates for these more recent years can be ordered online.

On 31 December 1854 or earlier: see parish registers

Ireland

Republic of Ireland

From 1845 onwards: see **www.irishgenealogy.ie** for birth register entries from 1864; marriages from 1845 (non-Roman Catholic) and marriages from 1864 (including Roman Catholic); and deaths from 1864. Online register access continues to be updated year by year, with a 100-closure period for birth registers, 75 years for marriages and 50 years for deaths.

1845/1864 and earlier: see parish registers

Northern Ireland

From 1845 onwards: Births, marriages and deaths registers for Northern Ireland can be accessed by **Irishgenealogy.ie** (as for the Republic) up to partition – 1922.

Birth certificates from 1864 onwards: **www.nidirect.gov.uk/services/order-birth-certificate-online**. Marriage certificates from 1845 onwards for non-Roman Catholics, 1864 onwards for Roman Catholic marriages: **www.nidirect.gov.uk/services/order-marriage-certificate-online**. Death certificates from 1864 onwards: **www.nidirect.gov.uk/services/order-death-certificate-online**

1845/1864 and earlier: see parish registers

Isle of Man

From 1849 onwards: find marriages from 1849 and births and deaths from 1878 on **www.manxbmd.com/** To order certificates see **www.gov.im/categories/births-deaths-and-marriages/**

Before 1849/1878: see parish registers

Channel Islands

Alderney

From 1850 onwards: find births and deaths from 1850 and marriages from 1886.The Priaulx Library holds microfilms of the indexes: **www.priaulxlibrary.co.uk/collections/family-history**

Before 1850/1886: see parish registers

Guernsey

From 1840 onwards: find births and deaths from 1840 and marriages from 1913. See Priaulx Library as above for microfilms indexes. See **https://societe.org.gg/wp/family-history/** for help

Before 1840/1913: see parish registers

Jersey

From August 1842 onwards: find births, marriages and deaths from 1842. See Priaulx Library as above for microfilms indexes. Also see **https://jerseyfamilyhistory.org/sources-of-research/** for useful information on ordering certificates

Before 1842: see parish registers

Sark

From 1925 onwards: find births, marriages and deaths from 1925. See Priaulx Library as above for microfilms indexes. Also see **https://jerseyfamilyhistory.org/sources-of-research/** for useful information on ordering certificates

Before 1925: see parish registers

Civil registration became compulsory at different dates and coverage can be partial. Download the free "Guide to Civil, Parish, and Census Records at the Priaulx Library" from **www.priaulxlibrary.co.uk/downloads**

Q I'd like to find my ancestor recorded in the birth/marriage/death indexes overseas, what can I do?

Find the most comprehensive online searchable index for BMDs for Canada at www.familysearch.org/search/collection/1520604

My ancestor was born/married/died in:

America

The BMD records are kept by each state and tend to date from the early 1900s. Some New England states started keeping records of BMDs at a town level three centuries earlier – in the 1600s.

- The FamilySearch Wiki gives a great overview of using BMD records for research in America: **www.familysearch.org/wiki/en/U.S._Vital_Records_Class_Handout**
- **www.archives.gov/research/vital-records** has nice useful overview information
- **http://familytr.ee/usavitalrecords** – this link is so handy – click on your state of interest and it will show you how to order BMD certificates, the cost for each, and pointers of where to search if the records you're after are outside the date range they cover.

Canada

There is not a centralised federal collection of BMD records, and the starting date for the records varies between say 1854 for birth records for British Columbia, to 1925 for the start of the BMD collections for the North West Territories.

- Searching of indexes and ordering of certificates are both steps that you take via the relevant province or territory – to find out more about the available records visit **www.bac-lac.gc.ca/eng/** – scroll down to "A to Z tools and guides" then select the guide for "Births, Marriages and Death recorded in Canada".

New Zealand

Search historical BMDs (with 100, 80 and 50 year closure periods for more recent BMD events respectively. Births and deaths from 1848, marriages from 1854).

- Find overview information at **http://familytr.ee/nzhistoricalbmd**
- Search indexes and order certificates online at **www.bdmhistoricalrecords.dia.govt.nz/Home/**

Australia

The BMD records are kept by each state. The starting point for the records varies from state to state, as does the information recorded on a BMD certificate.

- This web address has useful overview information, and on the left-hand side has links to each of the states: **www.nla.gov.au/research-guides/australian-birth-death-and-marriage-records**
- See also the eResources section of the National Library of Australia for links to library networked BMD indexes. Use the link above and follow the link to eResources

Rest of world

Great starting points are:

- **www.nationalarchives.gov.uk/help-with-your-research/research-guides/birth-marriage-death-sea-or-abroad/** for a guide and archive details about British BMDs abroad and at sea
- The Overseas & military BMD collection on TheGenealogist – find out about it here: **http://familytr.ee/tgoverseasbmds** (scroll down the page until you get to 'overseas')
- **www.cyndislist.com** followed by a forward slash and the name of the country you're interested in. E.g. **www.cyndislist.com/finland**
- **www.familysearch.org/wiki** – and search on the name of the country you're wishing to search for records in. e.g. South Africa: **www.familysearch.org/en/wiki/South_Africa_Civil_Registration**
- **www.ukbmd.org.uk/british_abroad** – for the British Abroad (has links to other records than BMDs too)

Q My ancestor was adopted, how do I find out about them?

Before the introduction of legally binding adoption, adoptions took place but were on an informal basis and the adoptive parents had no legal rights. If you are searching in these earlier periods (bulleted below) seek out records for workhouses, children's homes and the poor law for clues about possible adoptions arranged by these organisations.

- 1926 and earlier in England and Wales
- 30 September 1930 and earlier in Scotland
- 31 December 1930 and earlier in Northern Ireland
- 31 December 1953 and earlier in the Republic of Ireland

My ancestor was adopted in the 20th century:

My ancestor was adopted in England and Wales, on 1 January 1927 or later:
Find background info at **www.adoptionsearchreunion.org.uk/search/righttosearch/accessrecords.htm**

My ancestor was adopted in Scotland, on 1 October 1930 or later:
Explore the guide at **www.nrscotland.gov.uk/research/research-guides/research-guides-a-z/adoption-records**

My ancestor was adopted in the Republic of Ireland, on 1 January 1954 or later:
Find information to get started at **https://aai.gov.ie/**

My ancestor was adopted in Northern Ireland, after 1930:
To get started, see **http://familytr.ee/niadoption**

Official adoption records organised by local authorities and the establishment of Adopted Children's Registers only began in the early/mid 20th century in the British Isles and vary country to country.

I am adopted and wish to trace by birth family:
For England and Wales: **www.gov.uk/adoption-records**

Fascinating PhD on adoption in Ireland 1911-1971: **http://mural.maynoothuniversity.ie/4876/1/Colleen%20Stewart%20PhD.pdf**

Useful overview link: **https://www.family-tree.co.uk/how-to-guides/how-to-find-your-uk-ancestors-using-adoption-records/**

Q How can I trace the parish registers I need?

Unlike the statutory BMD collections we've covered above, parish registers of baptisms, marriages and burials aren't available in one centralised place for England. It is also worth remembering that parish registers can be older records too (so some may not have survived). Bishop's Transcripts (copies of parish registers submitted to the diocese) may have survived where a parish register might not.

Yes I know the place I need to search for my ancestor.

England
Useful leads for parish registers include family history societies (which may have transcribed the records and provide online access via a members' area), the local archives and the Society of Genealogists, **www.sog.org.uk**. The major subscription websites also increasingly provide collections of parish registers. Note that the online records are often arranged by county and date spans of records covered vary.

Scotland
Find the Old Parochial Registers (OPR) 1553-1855, Roman Catholic and other church registers for Scotland at **http://familytr.ee/scotopr**

Wales
Find parish registers for 500 parishes in the National Library of Wales on microfilm or digitised at Ancestry and Findmypast; pre-1837 Nonconformist registers are held at The National Archives, Kew, or digitised at TheGenealogist.

Ireland
Find registers for the majority of Roman Catholic parishes Ireland up to 1880 at **https://registers.nli.ie/**; find Church of Ireland records in the (work in progress) Anglican Record Project at **www.ireland.anglican.org/about/rcb-library/anglican-record-project**; and Presbyterian records at the Public Record Office of Northern Ireland. RootsIreland.ie has widespread baptism, marriage, burial (and other) records up to 1923.
TIP: to see the coverage for your county of interest before subscribing go to RootsIreland.ie, click on 'Search by county', choose the county of interest to you, then click on 'Online sources' – and a table of available records via parish will be displayed.

No, I don't know the place I need to search for my ancestor in the parish registers.

In this case you need websites where you can search widely. For Scotland, Ireland and Wales there are the websites mentioned just previously, which have good coverage for each country. For England the parish registers aren't all available on any single website. Explore the following sites, each of which covers many places, but not all:

- **www.freereg.org.uk** – for transcripts of baptism, marriage and burial records for England, Wales, Scotland and Ireland but it is a work in progress with partial coverage. That said the website does hold nearly 50 million transcribed records.
- **www.ancestry.co.uk** – see a list of UK parish registers available here: **www.ancestry.co.uk/search/categories/epr/**
- **www.findmypast.co.uk** – with records for Britain and Ireland, for baptisms see **http://familytr.ee/fmpbaptisms**; marriages **http://familytr.ee/fmpmarriages**; and burials **http://familytr.ee/fmpburials**
- **www.thegenealogist.co.uk** – in addition to the parish record books see the non-parochial records, e.g. for Nonconformist ancestors **www.thegenealogist.co.uk/search/advanced/bmd/non-conformist/**
- **www.familysearch.org** – with international coverage you can explore ancestral life events globally.
- **www parishregister.co.uk**
- **https://sogdata.org.uk/** (Society of Genealogists' online data for members)

Help, I just can't find my ancestor in the parish registers.

Yes, I've checked that:

- the registers survive for the period I'm interested in
- that the record collection I'm searching online doesn't have any years missing

If so, then other options to try include tracking down Bishop's Transcripts, Nonconformist & overseas BMD records.

No, I've not checked that the registers survive for the period I'm interested in, nor I have I checked the coverage of the record collection of the website I'm searching on.

To check for parish register coverage, see:

For England

The map and boundaries website, covering England, also provides details about the dates from which parish registers and Bishop's Transcripts date: **www.familysearch.org/mapp/**. Phillimore's Index does a similar job in book form.

For Scotland

Useful background information to the coverage of Old Parochial Registers at **www.nrscotland.gov.uk/research/guides/old-parish-registers/list-of-old-parish-registers**

For Ireland

A colour-coded table of what survives and where it's held compiled by the excellent Claire Santry: **www.irishancestors.ie/resources/unique-resources/church-of-ireland-parish-records-list/**

For Wales

The National Library of Wales advised, 'for dates of surviving parish registers see *Cofrestri Plwyf Cymru/Parish Registers of Wales* eds. C J Williams and J Watts-Williams (NLW, Aberystwyth, 2000)'.

Checking a website's record collection coverage:

Some websites provide more information, more clearly, about their record collections than others. Be sure to read the notes and ascertain the source of the information that you're searching. Note whether any date spans are mentioned and any missing years that are noted. From the source information given you can follow this up on the relevant archive's website or online catalogue, where you might be able to learn more about the record collection (both what's survived, and what hasn't, for instance).

We hope you find this handy as a starting point to thinking about where to look.

Whether the record you're after was kept in the first place, has survived the passage of time, or made it into an indexing or digitisation project are all matters that will have a massive impact on what you'll find and where you need to look, but we wish you luck in your research.

HOW TO SPOT CLUES IN BIRTH, MARRIAGE AND DEATH CERTIFICATES

Birth, marriage and death certificates are very useful for piecing together your family tree because:

- they are nationwide records (ie the vast majority of our ancestors will have been recorded)
- they have been kept since the mid-1800s (so you can use these records to trace your family tree over approximately a 170-year period)
- they include lots of details so you can identify your ancestors and find further clues to other relations.

Examine these examples of a birth, marriage and death certificate below and see how many family history clues they hold!

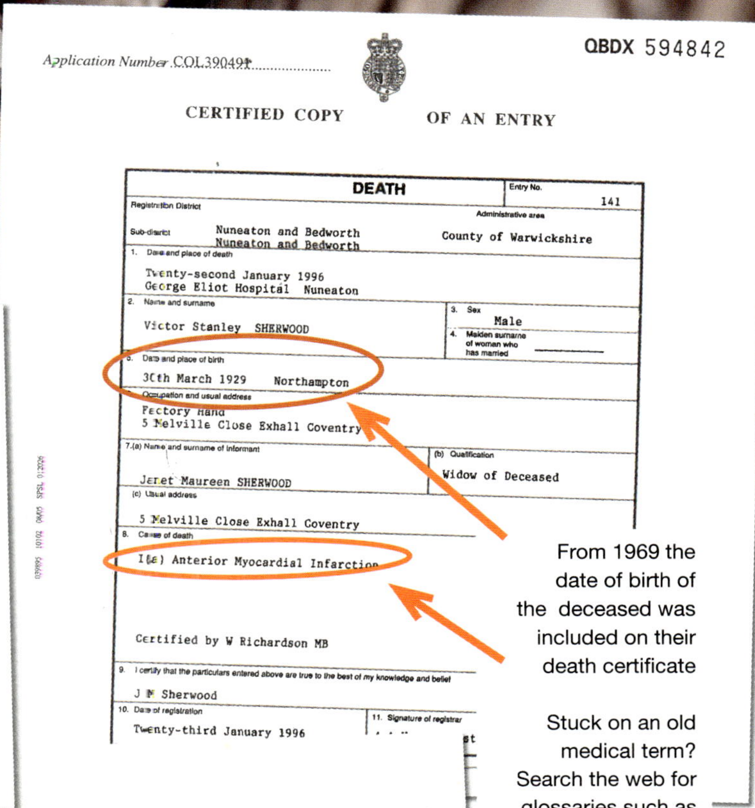

Application Number COL39049
QBDX 594842
CERTIFIED COPY OF AN ENTRY

DEATH		Entry No. 141
Registration District		Administrative area
Sub-district: Nuneaton and Bedworth, Nuneaton and Bedworth		County of Warwickshire
1. Date and place of death: Twenty-second January 1996, George Eliot Hospital Nuneaton		
2. Name and surname: Victor Stanley SHERWOOD	3. Sex: Male	4. Maiden surname of woman who has married:
5. Date and place of birth: 30th March 1929 Northampton		
6. Occupation and usual address: Factory Hand, 5 Melville Close Exhall Coventry		
7.(a) Name and surname of informant: Janet Maureen SHERWOOD	(b) Qualification: Widow of Deceased	
(c) Usual address: 5 Melville Close Exhall Coventry		
8. Cause of death: I(a) Anterior Myocardial Infarction. Certified by W Richardson MB		
9. I certify that the particulars entered above are true to the best of my knowledge and belief: J M Sherwood		
10. Date of registration: Twenty-third January 1996	11. Signature of registrar	

From 1969 the date of birth of the deceased was included on their death certificate

Stuck on an old medical term? Search the web for glossaries such as **www.thornber.net/medicine/html/medgloss.html**

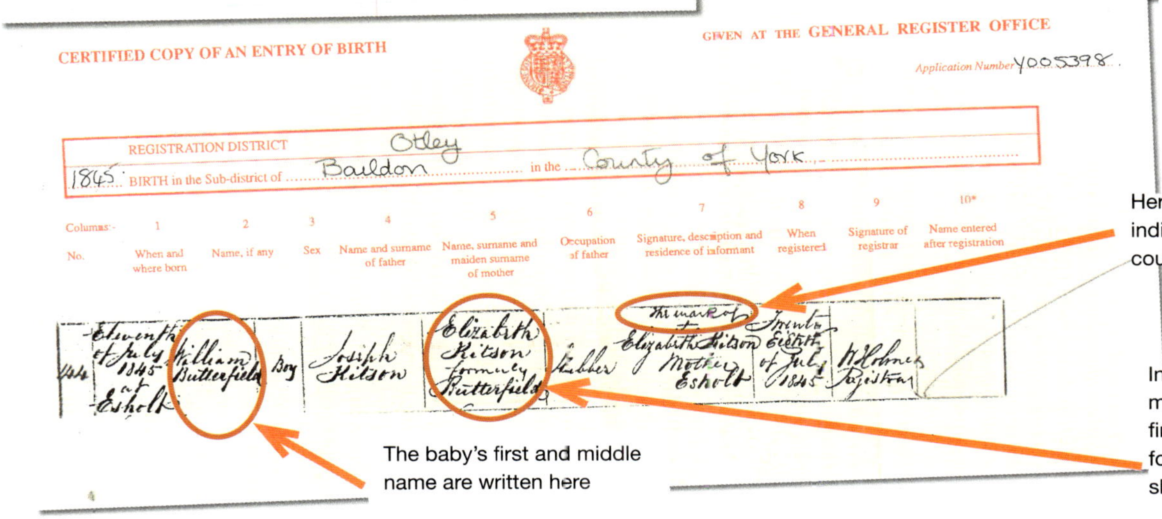

CERTIFIED COPY OF AN ENTRY OF BIRTH — GIVEN AT THE GENERAL REGISTER OFFICE

Application Number Y005398

REGISTRATION DISTRICT Otley

1845 BIRTH in the Sub-district of Baildon in the County of York

Columns: No.	1 When and where born	2 Name, if any	3 Sex	4 Name and surname of father	5 Name, surname and maiden surname of mother	6 Occupation of father	7 Signature, description and residence of informant	8 When registered	9 Signature of registrar	10* Name entered after registration
444	Eleventh of July 1845 at Esholt	William Butterfield	Boy	Joseph Hitson	Elizabeth Hitson formerly Butterfield	Fuller	The mark of Elizabeth Hitson Mother Esholt	Twenty Eighth of July 1845	W Holmes Registrar	

Here is stated 'The mark of' indicating that the mother could not write her name

In the box for the mother's name you may find her maiden name or former married name, if she's been married before

The baby's first and middle name are written here

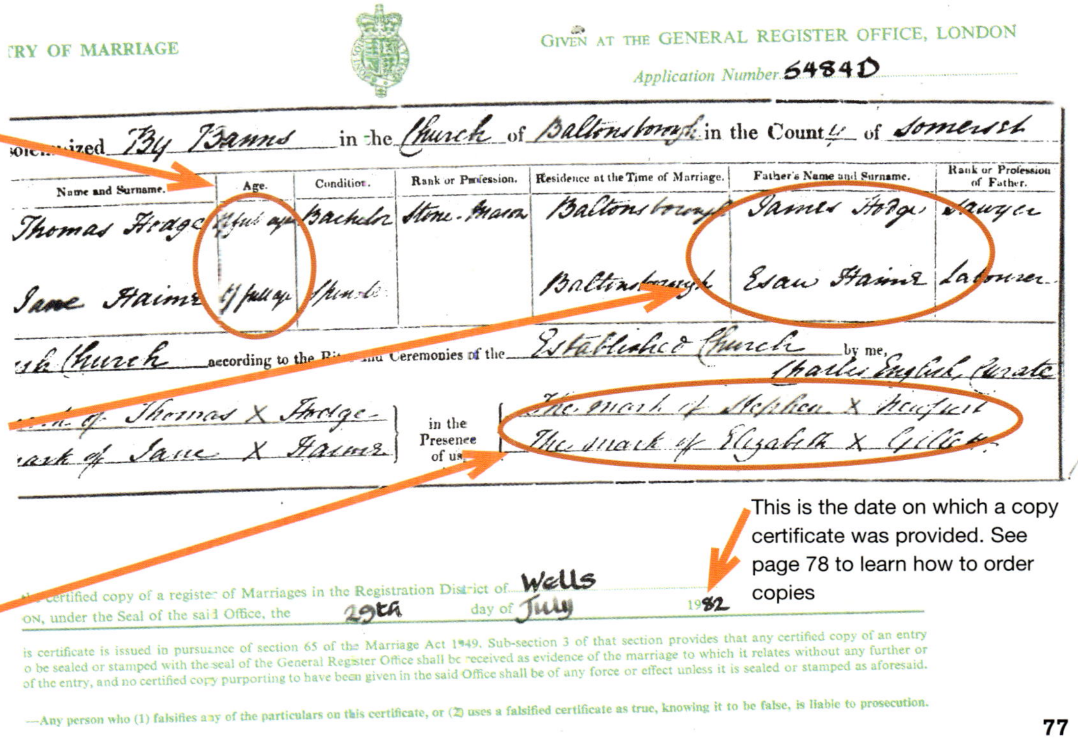

…TRY OF MARRIAGE — GIVEN AT THE GENERAL REGISTER OFFICE, LONDON

Application Number 6484D

…solemnized By Banns in the Church of Baltonsborough in the County of Somerset

Name and Surname.	Age.	Condition.	Rank or Profession.	Residence at the Time of Marriage.	Father's Name and Surname.	Rank or Profession of Father.
Thomas Hodge	Of full age	Bachelor	Stone Mason	Baltonsborough	James Hodge	Sawyer
Jane Haine	Of full age	Spinster		Baltonsborough	Esau Haine	Labourer

…sh Church according to the Rites and Ceremonies of the Established Church by me, Charles English Curate

…mark of Thomas X Hodge; …mark of Jane X Haine — in the Presence of us, The mark of Stephen X Hayfield; The mark of Elizabeth X Gillett

…certified copy of a register of Marriages in the Registration District of Wells … under the Seal of the said Office, the 29th day of July 1982

…is certificate is issued in pursuance of section 65 of the Marriage Act 1949. Sub-section 3 of that section provides that any certified copy of an entry …o be sealed or stamped with the seal of the General Register Office shall be received as evidence of the marriage to which it relates without any further or …of the entry, and no certified copy purporting to have been given in the said Office shall be of any force or effect unless it is sealed or stamped as aforesaid.

—Any person who (1) falsifies any of the particulars on this certificate, or (2) uses a falsified certificate as true, knowing it to be false, is liable to prosecution.

'Of full age' means 21 years or older

The names and occupations of the fathers of the couple to be married should be included, so providing you with the start of another generation of your family tree. Scottish records include mother's names.

Be sure to note the witnesses' names – sometimes you may realise that they are family members

This is the date on which a copy certificate was provided. See page 78 to learn how to order copies

HOW TO ORDER *BMD CERTIFICATES ONLINE*

England & Wales

To order the certificate for a birth, marriage or death that occurred in England and Wales, you will need to know the volume and page number of the birth, marriage or death register index in which your ancestor's event was recorded. It's not as complicated as it sounds however, as the birth, marriage and death indexes for England and Wales are available on several sites, and go back to the start of civil registration in these countries (1 July 1837).

Here we're going to explore the FreeBMD.org.uk website.

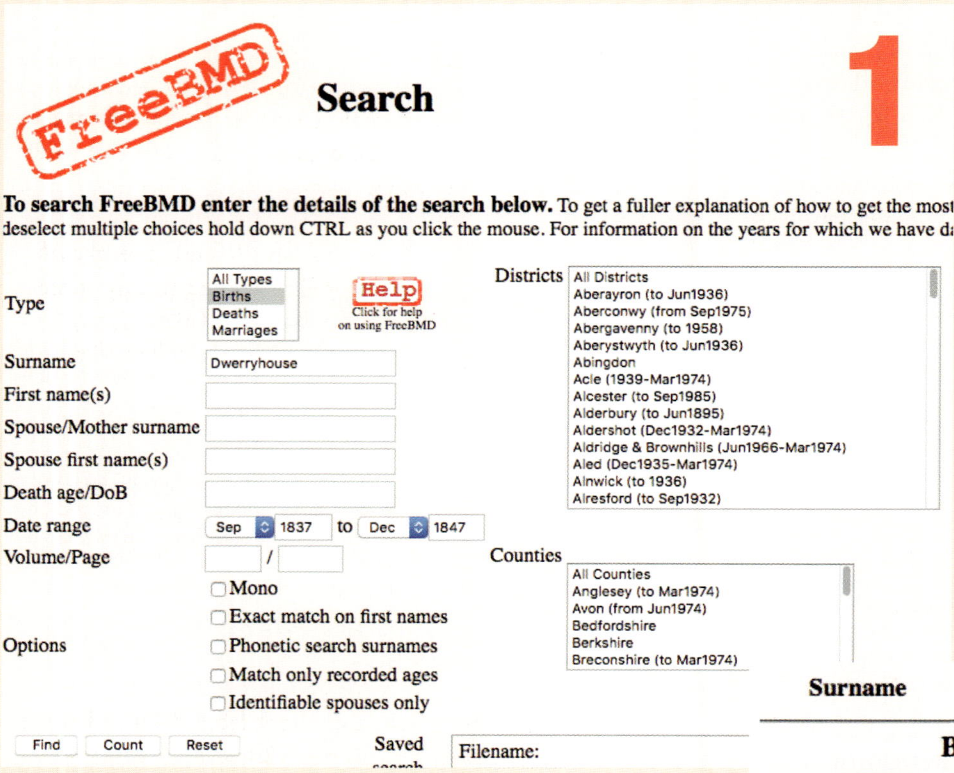

1 Go to **www.freebmd.org.uk** Enter your search terms, experimenting with record type, place, date spans, as well as ancestor names.

Mar, Jun, Sep & Dec

In the date range you will see that the months stated are Mar, Jun, Sep and Dec. These refer to the quarters, i.e. a birth registered in January, Feburary or March will be in the Mar quarter.

Note too that the birth of a baby born in late February may not have been registered until April, in which case that birth will be registered in the Jun quarter.

Surname	First name(s)	District	Vol	Page
	Births Dec 1837 (>99%)			
DWERRYHOUSE	William	Prescot	20	395
	Births Jun 1838 (>99%)			
DWERRYHOUSE	Thomas	Prescot	20	640
	Births Dec 1838 (>99%)			
DWERRYHOUSE	Elizabeth	Prescot	20	605

2 You will see that the index has far fewer details than the actual certificate (compare the certificates on page 77 of the *Family History Workbook for Beginners*).

It is this reason that it can be worth the time and expense to track down and order a certificate – to get the full details about your ancestor. When you find an entry that you suspect to be your ancestor, be sure to note the volume and page reference, which will come in helpful when ordering your certificate.

When looking at the top entry in the example shown right, the volume is 20 and the page number is 395.

3

Go to **www.gro.gov.uk/gro/content** and click on 'Order certificates online'. PDFs of register entries are available for access within about 4 days costing £7 each: births from 1837, deaths from 1837, no marriages. Certificated paper copies of the register entries are also available for births, marriages and deaths, £11 each. The jpegs, pdfs and certificated paper copies each provide the same details for family history purposes, so there is no advantage to spending more. They are all generally referred to by family historians as the birth, marriage and death certificates.

Register to set up an account with GRO, then place your order.

Scotland

To order the certificate for a birth, marriage or death that occurred in Scotland, you will need to visit ScotlandsPeople.gov.uk. Here you will be able to search and obtain digitised copies of register entries for births over 100 years ago, marriages over 75 years ago and deaths over 50 years ago. For more recent years you will need to order copies which will be sent to you by post.

1

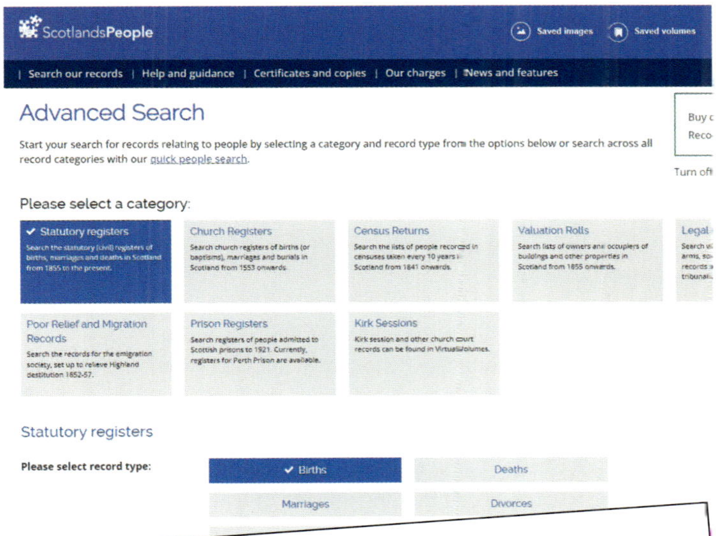

2

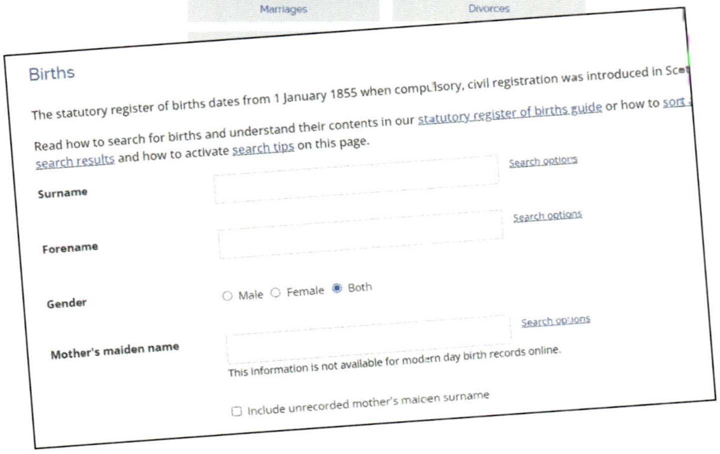

1 Go to **www.scotlandspeople.gov.uk** and register (or log in if you have already created an account). Select: Search Our Records / People Search / Statutory Records / then Births, Marriages or Deaths

2 Experiment with your search terms: for instance, the place options and date ranges. Consider whether your ancestor may have used an alternative first name, or may the surname have been spelt in various ways.

3 When you have found an entry of interest you will need to buy some credits (in batches, from £7.50). It costs 6 credits (£1.50) to view a register entry.

Scottish register entries

Buy credits to download Scottish register entries at ScotlandsPeople. Historic records are available to download immediately; for more recent records you will need to order a certificate (priced £12).

Ireland

Civil registration records for Ireland were kept from 1845 for non-Roman Catholic marriages. All births, all deaths and all other marriages were kept from 1864. Historic registers are freely available to view online at **www.irishgenealogy.ie/**.

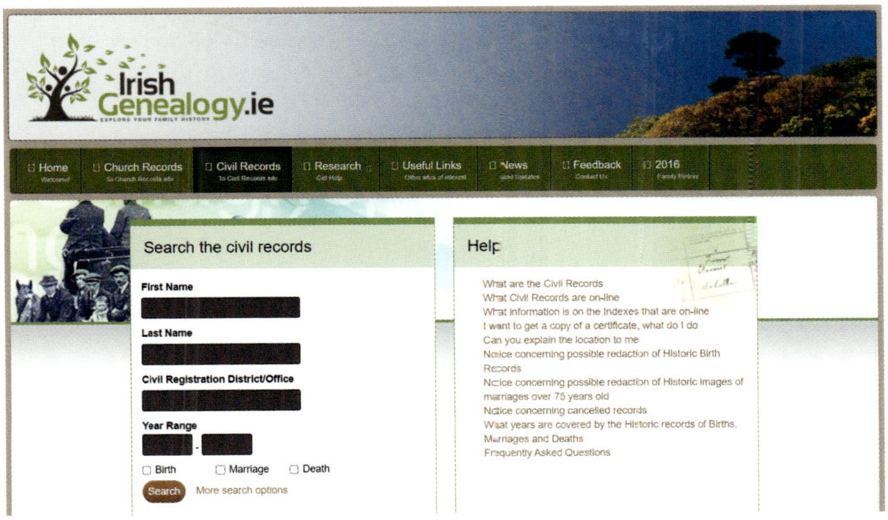

1 Go to **www.irishgenealogy.ie** and select 'Civil Registration' and start your search.Before viewing the results you will need to read the terms and conditions and enter your name to agree that you are using the website appropriately.

2 From the list of search results, click on the name of your person of interest

3 If available select 'Image' to view, for free, a digitised copy of the register page. If not available you may need to order a copy, priced 5 Euros.

Irish register entries

Remember that from 1922 the records for Northern Ireland and Eire were kept by different General Register Offices. See page the BMD finding aid (page 73 of the *Workbook*) for details, including for post-1922 Northern Ireland, and ones for Eire too. This website (left) only has historic records.

How to search and use the census

The census can give a rich snapshot of your family's life decade by decade, such as where and how they lived, members of their household, occupations, approximate ages and birthplaces too.

The 1911 Census reveals extra details, such as how long a couple were married and how many children they'd had. It's the last census taken before the First World War, so it is particularly moving to see so many men who lost their lives recorded with their families, in happier times and in peacetime occupations. The 1921 Census reveals a post-war world, with many orphans and unemployed people.

The earlier censuses are also extremely interesting, providing information about our ancestors as individuals, and also about the communities they lived and worked in.

In this guide we'll look at examples of different census documents over the decades, and from each of the four countries of the British Isles: Scotland, England, Wales and Ireland.

What years of the census can be searched?

The first census returns for the British Isles were taken in 1801, but the early years of the census tended not to record the names of individual people – they just recorded total numbers of people (ie good information for statisticians, but no good for finding your named ancestor).

However, from the 1841 Census onwards the name of each person was recorded, and this continued every ten years, 1851, 1861, 1871, etc. To protect people's privacy the census details of individuals are not released for a century after each census was taken. Consequently the most recent census available to family historians is the 1921 Census for England and Wales and Scotland. The next census to become available will be the 1926 Census for Eire, the 1931 Census for Scotland and the 1951 Census for England and Wales. So you can see that the release of a new census collection is relatively infrequent treat.

So, for England, Wales and Scotland you can currently search for ancestors in the decennial censuses (ie every 10 years) from 1841 to 1921. For Ireland, the only complete censuses are those for 1901 and 1911.

Key census abbreviations

Of the commonly found census abbreviations, the ones relating to birth places are most typically found on the 1841 Census, rather than the later ones.

MS - male servant

FS - female servant

Y - yes (as in 'yes' that person was born in the county)

N - no (as in 'no' that person wasn't born in the county)

S - Scotland (as a birthplace for someone born in Scotland, but who is on the census subsequently of a different country)

I - Ireland - as above

F - Foreign parts - as above

Ag Lab - agricultural labourer

Un - unmarried

M - married

W - widowed

Do – Ditto

NK – not known

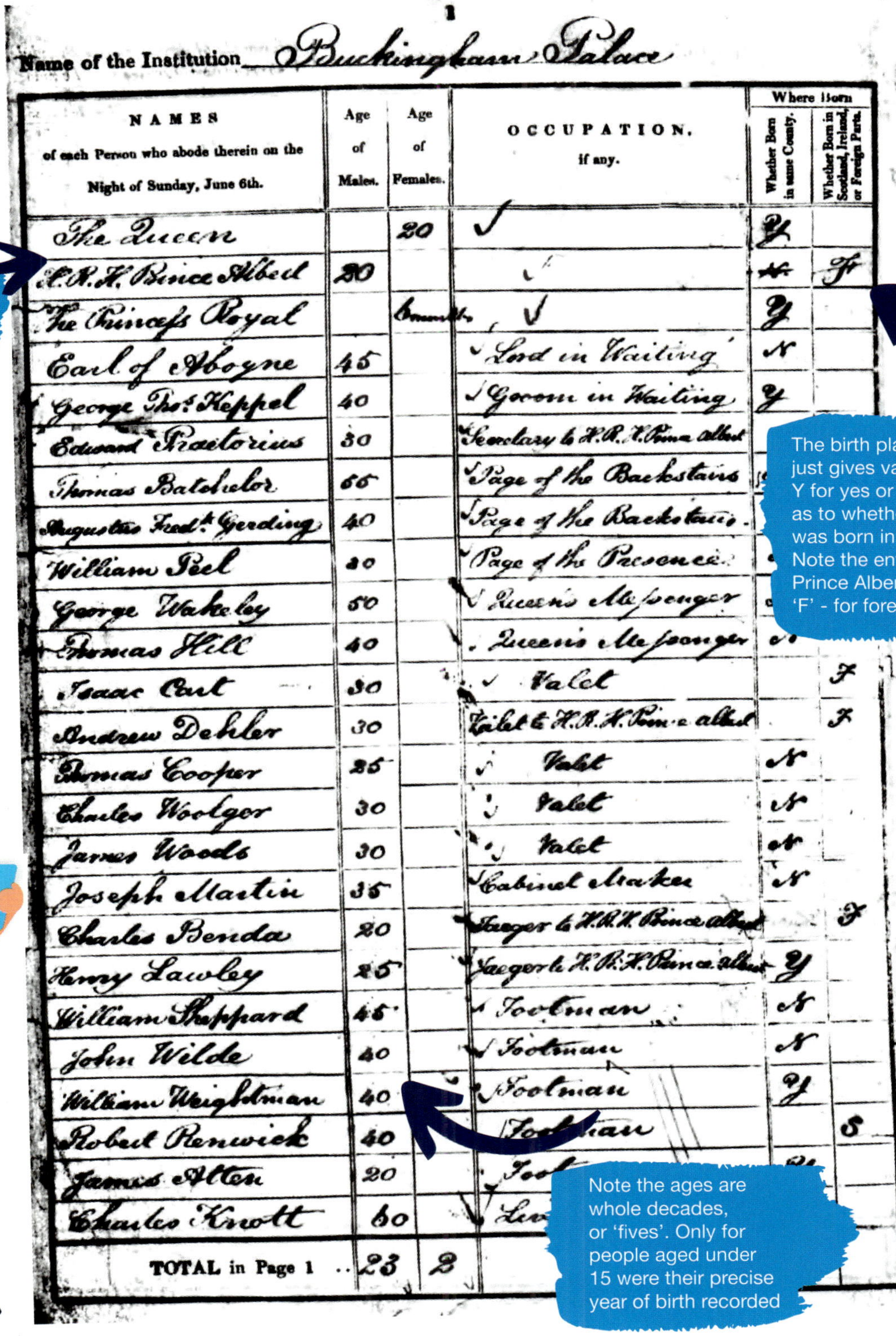

Name of the Institution *Buckingham Palace*

NAMES of each Person who abode therein on the Night of Sunday, June 6th.	Age of Males.	Age of Females.	OCCUPATION, if any.	Whether Born in same County.	Whether Born in Scotland, Ireland, or Foreign Parts.
The Queen		20	✓	Y	
H.R.H. Prince Albert	20		✓	N	F
The Princess Royal		6 month	✓	Y	
Earl of Aboyne	45		Lord in Waiting	N	
George Thos Keppel	40		Groom in Waiting	Y	
Edward Praetorius	30		Secretary to H.R.H. Prince Albert		
Thomas Batchelor	65		Page of the Backstairs		
Augustus Fredk Gerding	40		Page of the Backstairs		
William Peel	40		Page of the Presence		
George Wakeley	50		Queen's Messenger		
Thomas Hill	40		Queen's Messenger	N	
Isaac Cart	30		Valet		F
Andrew Dehler	30		Valet to H.R.H. Prince Albert		F
Thomas Cooper	25		Valet	N	
Charles Woolger	30		Valet	N	
James Woods	30		Valet	N	
Joseph Martin	35		Cabinet Maker	N	
Charles Benda	20		Jaeger to H.R.H. Prince Albert		F
Henry Lawley	25		Jaeger to H.R.H. Prince Albert	Y	
William Sheppard	45		Footman	N	
John Wilde	40		Footman	N	
William Weightman	40		Footman	Y	
Robert Renwick	40		Footman		S
James Alten	20		Foo[illegible]	[illegible]	
Charles Knott	60		Liv[illegible]		
TOTAL in Page 1	23	2			

This entry shows Queen Victoria and her husband Prince Albert

The birth place column just gives vague clues: Y for yes or N for no, as to whether a person was born in the county. Note the entry for Prince Albert. stating 'F' - for foreign parts

Note the ages are whole decades, or 'fives'. Only for people aged under 15 were their precise year of birth recorded

The 1841 Census

For the earliest census of use to family historians – the 1841 Census – the details included were:

- The borough
- The parish
- The street name (usually no street numbers)
- Whether the house was uninhabited or inhabited
- The name of each person living there on the preceding night
- The age and sex of each person (this was supposed to be the exact age for people up to 15 years old, and to be rounded down to the nearest 5 years for those who were older)
- The occupation
- Whether or not the person was born in the county (simply marked 'Y' for yes, or 'N' for no)
- Whether the person was born in England/Scotland, Ireland or Foreign Parts (simply marked 'S', 'I' or 'F')

With the 1851 Census two very useful details were added to the census forms: relationship to head of household and a more specific birth place.

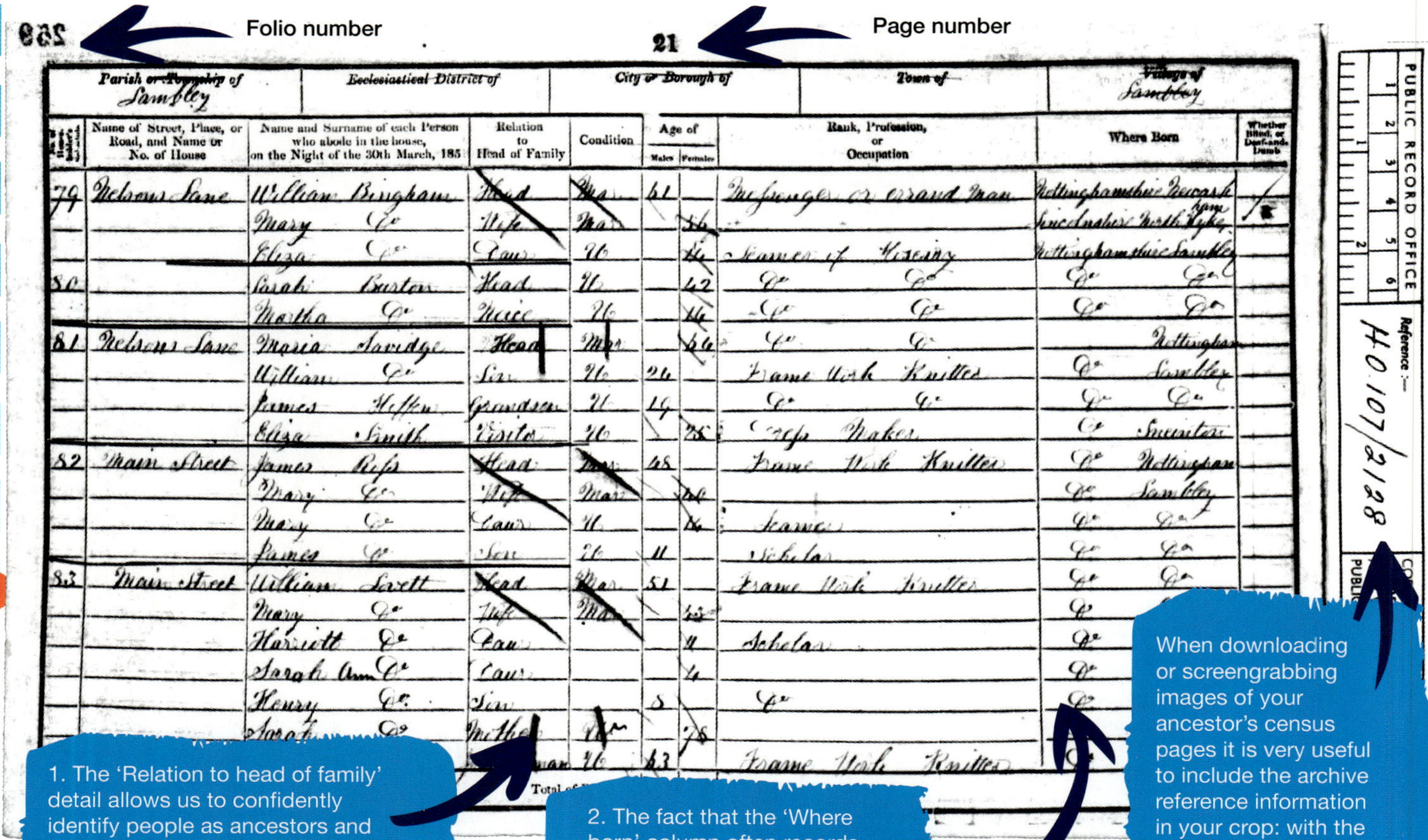

No.	Street / House	Name	Relation	Condition	Males	Females	Occupation	Where Born
79	Nelsons Lane	William Bingham	Head	Mar	61		Messenger or errand Man	Nottinghamshire Newark
		Mary Do	Wife	Mar		56		Lincolnshire North Hyke
		Eliza Do	Daur	U		16	Seamer of Hosiery	Nottinghamshire Lambley
80		Sarah Burton	Head	U		42	Do Do	Do Do
		Martha Do	Niece	U		16	Do Do	Do Do
81	Nelsons Lane	Maria Savidge	Head	Mar		56	Do Do	Nottingham
		William Do	Son	U	26		Frame Work Knitter	Do Lambley
		James Heffen	Grandson	U	19		Do Do	Do Do
		Eliza Smith	Visitor	U		25	Cap Maker	Do Sneinton
82	Main Street	James Ross	Head	Mar	48		Frame Work Knitter	Do Nottingham
		Mary Do	Wife	Mar		46		Do Lambley
		Mary Do	Daur	U		16	Seamer	Do Do
		James Do	Son	U	11		Scholar	Do Do
83	Main Street	William Lovett	Head	Mar	51		Frame Work Knitter	Do Do
		Mary Do	Wife	Mar		52		Do
		Harriett Do	Daur			9	Scholar	Do
		Sarah Ann Do	Daur			4		Do
		Henry Do	Son		5		Do	Do
		Sarah Do	Mother	W		76		

1. The 'Relation to head of family' detail allows us to confidently identify people as ancestors and add them to our family tree in the correct places. Without this detail it is possible to muddle people with the same surnames (for instance confusing a nephew for a son or a sister for a wife).

2. The fact that the 'Where born' column often records a town or village gives us a much more specific location to track down our ancestors in other records, such as birth, marriage and death records, and parish registers.

When downloading or screengrabbing images of your ancestor's census pages it is very useful to include the archive reference information in your crop: with the series, piece, folio and page number. This will enable you or other people to precisely identify whereabouts the page was found in the future.

30/03/1851 LINTON, JAMES (Census 1851 810/00 001/00 005)

© Crown Copyright, Image was generated at 15 July 2016 14:57

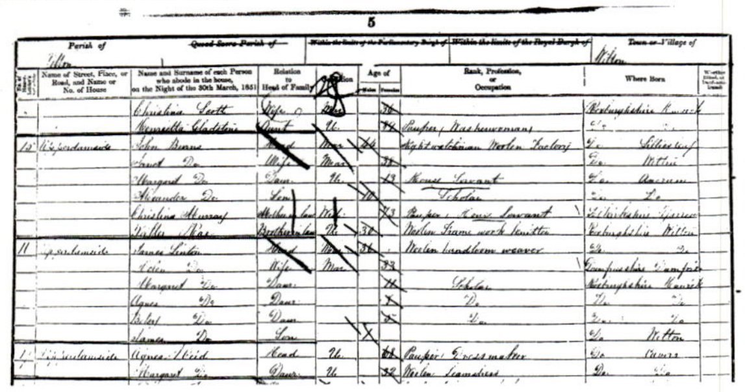

Census markings

When looking at a census page you might notice handwritten slashes.

A double slash - // - indicates a new household (remember that several households might live in one building).

Other scribbles will largely just be the marks of the enumerator and statisticians who worked on the documents.

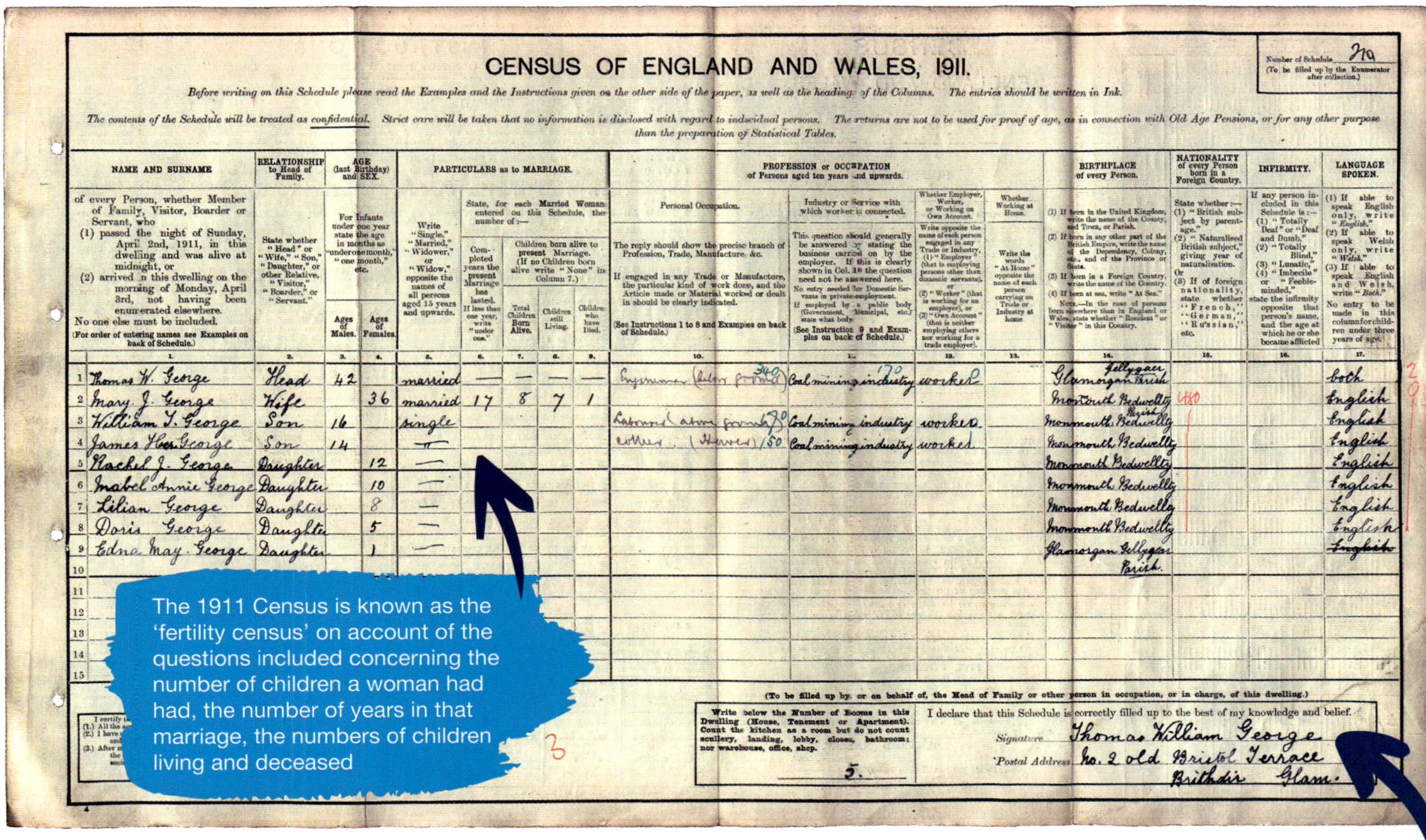

CENSUS OF ENGLAND AND WALES, 1911.

Before writing on this Schedule please read the Examples and the Instructions given on the other side of the paper, as well as the headings of the Columns. The entries should be written in Ink.

The contents of the Schedule will be treated as confidential. Strict care will be taken that no information is disclosed with regard to individual persons. The returns are not to be used for proof of age, as in connection with Old Age Pensions, or for any other purpose than the preparation of Statistical Tables.

	Name and Surname	Relationship to Head of Family	Age (Males)	Age (Females)	Particulars as to Marriage	Years married	Children born alive	Children still living	Children who have died	Personal Occupation	Industry or Service	Employer, Worker or Own Account	Birthplace	Language Spoken
1	Thomas W. George	Head	42		married						Coal mining industry	worker	Glamorgan Gellygaer	both
2	Mary J. George	Wife		36	married	17	8	7	1				Monmouth Bedwellty	English
3	William T. George	Son	16		single						Coal mining industry	worker	Monmouth Bedwellty	English
4	James H. George	Son	14								Coal mining industry	worker	Monmouth Bedwellty	English
5	Rachel J. George	Daughter		12									Monmouth Bedwellty	English
6	Mabel Annie George	Daughter		10									Monmouth Bedwellty	English
7	Lilian George	Daughter		8									Monmouth Bedwellty	English
8	Doris George	Daughter		5									Monmouth Bedwellty	English
9	Edna May George	Daughter		1									Glamorgan Gellygaer	English

Write below the Number of Rooms in this Dwelling (House, Tenement or Apartment). Count the kitchen as a room but do not count scullery, landing, lobby, closet, bathroom; nor warehouse, office, shop. 5.

I declare that this Schedule is correctly filled up to the best of my knowledge and belief.

Signature Thomas William George

Postal Address No. 2 Old Bristol Terrace Brithdir Glam.

The 1911 Census is known as the 'fertility census' on account of the questions included concerning the number of children a woman had had, the number of years in that marriage, the numbers of children living and deceased

See your ancestor's handwriting on the 1911 Census on the original paperwork, usually filled in by the head of the household

The 1911 Census (England & Wales)

The 1911 Census is currently the most detailed census available to family historians.
The details included on this census are:

- The name of each person
- Their relationship to the head of the family
- The age and gender of each person
- The marital status
- For each married woman the number of years they have been married to their present spouse is included, as is the number of children born to that couple, with a break down of number still living, and the number of children who have died
- Occupation
- Industry
- Whether employer, worker, self-employed
- Place of birth
- Nationality
- And Infirmity (ie deaf, deaf and dumb, blind, lunatic, imbecile, feeble minded) – These can be upsetting terms for today's family historian to read about their ancestor, as, being a record from over a century ago, the census records the words used at the time.

The 1911 Census (Ireland)

While it is a huge challenge for family researchers that so many of the Irish census years have not survived the passage of time, they do have the advantage that the records that do survive are available to search free of charge (see the website listings on the final page). Be sure to check whether the counties that you're searching in have survived. Only a minority have for earlier Irish census records but they are a boon if your area is covered.

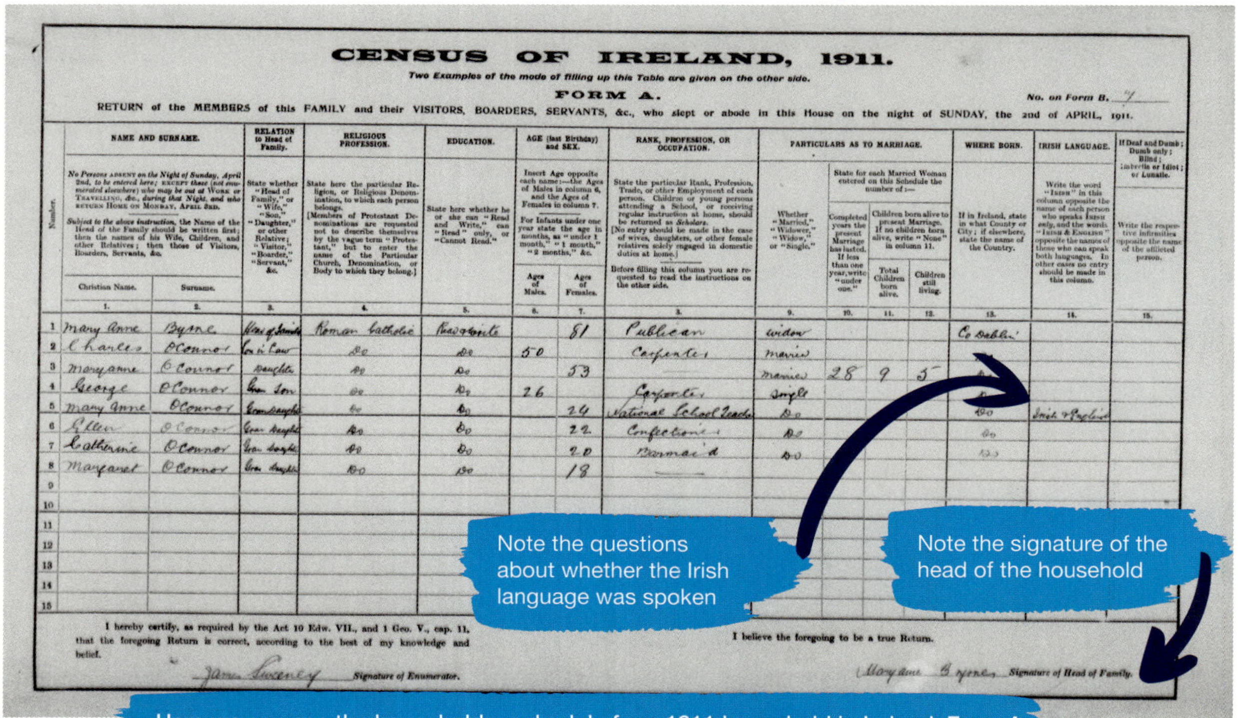

CENSUS OF IRELAND, 1911.

Two Examples of the mode of filling up this Table are given on the other side.

FORM A.

No. on Form B. 7

RETURN of the MEMBERS of this FAMILY and their VISITORS, BOARDERS, SERVANTS, &c., who slept or abode in this House on the night of SUNDAY, the 2nd of APRIL, 1911.

No.	Christian Name	Surname	Relation to Head of Family	Religious Profession	Education	Age (Males)	Age (Females)	Rank, Profession, or Occupation	Married, Widower, Widow, or Single	Completed years of present Marriage	Children born alive	Children still living	Where Born	Irish Language	If Deaf and Dumb; Dumb only; Blind; Imbecile or Idiot; or Lunatic
1	Mary Anne	Byrne	Head of Family	Roman Catholic	Read & write		81	Publican	Widow				Co Dublin		
2	Charles	O'Connor	Son in Law	Do	Do	50		Carpenter	Married						
3	Mary Anne	O'Connor	Daughter	Do	Do		53		Married	28	9	5			
4	George	O'Connor	Gran Son	Do	Do	26		Carpenter	Single						
5	Mary Anne	O'Connor	Grand daughter	Do	Do		24	National School Teacher	Do				Do	Irish & English	
6	Ellen	O'Connor	Gran daughter	Do	Do		22	Confectioner	Do				Do		
7	Catherine	O'Connor	Gran daughter	Do	Do		20	Barmaid	Do				Do		
8	Margaret	O'Connor	Gran daughter	Do	Do		18								

I hereby certify, as required by the Act 10 Edw. VII., and 1 Geo. V., cap. 11, that the foregoing Return is correct, according to the best of my knowledge and belief.

James Sweeney — Signature of Enumerator.

I believe the foregoing to be a true Return.

Mary Anne Byrne — Signature of Head of Family.

Here we can see the householder schedule for a 1911 household in Ireland: Form A

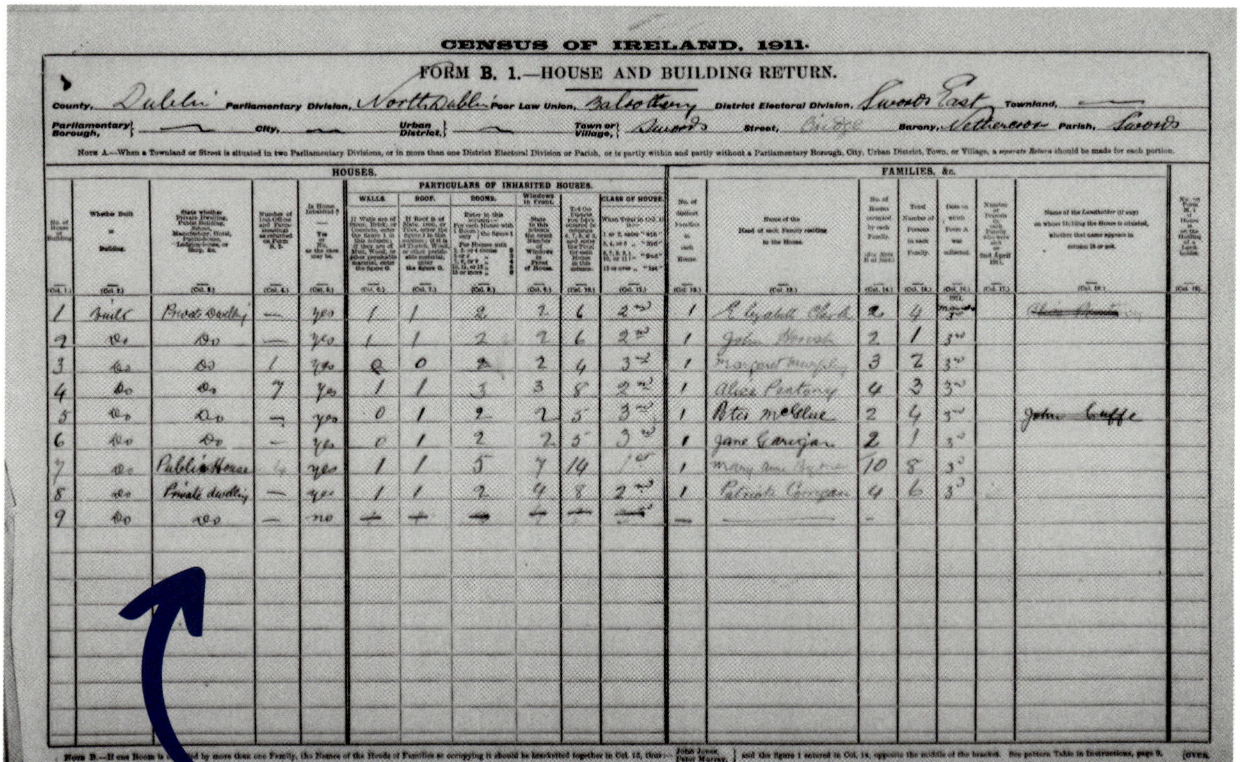

CENSUS OF IRELAND, 1911.

FORM B. 1.—HOUSE AND BUILDING RETURN.

County, Dublin. Parliamentary Division, North Dublin. Poor Law Union, Balrothery. District Electoral Division, Swords East. Townland, —. Parliamentary Borough, —. City, —. Urban District, —. Town or Village, Swords. Street, Bridge. Barony, Nethercross. Parish, Swords.

No. of House or Building	Whether Built or Building	State whether Private Dwelling, Public Building, School, Manufactory, Hotel, Public-house, Lodging-house, or Shop, &c.	Number of Out-Offices and Farm-steadings	Is House Inhabited?	Walls	Roof	Rooms	Windows in Front	Total	Class of House	No. of distinct Families in each House	Name of the Head of each Family residing in the House	No. of Rooms occupied by each Family	Total Number of Persons in each Family	Date on which Form A was collected	Name of the Landholder (if any)
1	Built	Private Dwelling	—	Yes	1	1	2	2	6	2nd	1	Elizabeth Clark	2	4	3rd	
2	Do	Do	—	Yes	1	1	2	2	6	2nd	1	John Bennett	2	1	3rd	
3	Do	Do	1	Yes	2	0	2	2	4	3rd	1	Margaret Murphy	3	2	3rd	
4	Do	Do	7	Yes	1	1	3	3	8	2nd	1	Alice Pentony	4	3	3rd	
5	Do	Do	—	Yes	0	1	2	2	5	3rd	1	Peter McGlue	2	4	3rd	John Cuffe
6	Do	Do	—	Yes	0	1	2	2	5	3rd	1	Jane Carrigan	2	1	3rd	
7	Do	Public House	4	Yes	1	1	5	7	14	1st	1	Mary Anne Byrne	10	8	3rd	
8	Do	Private dwelling	—	Yes	1	1	2	4	8	2nd	1	Patrick Corrigan	4	6	3rd	
9	Do	Do	—	no	—	—	—	—	—	—	—	—	—			

Form B gives details of each property: numbers of rooms, outbuildings etc

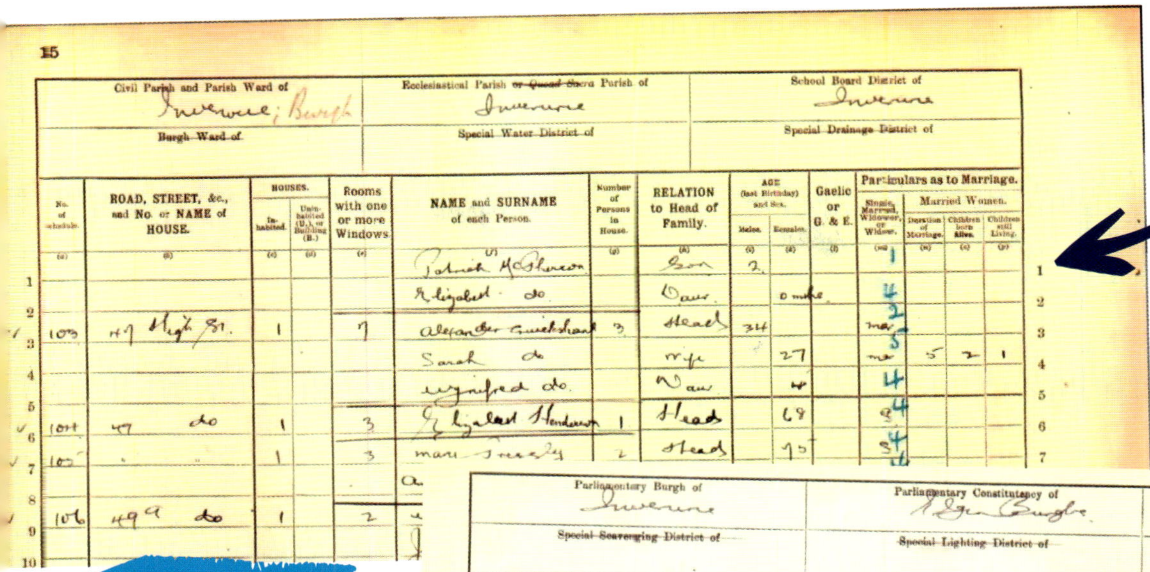

15

No. of schedule	ROAD, STREET, &c., and No. or NAME of HOUSE	HOUSES. Inhabited	Uninhabited (U.), or Building (B.)	Rooms with one or more Windows	NAME and SURNAME of each Person	Number of Persons in House	RELATION to Head of Family	AGE Males	AGE Females	Gaelic or G. & E.	Single, Married, Widower, or Widow	Duration of Marriage	Children born Alive	Children still Living

Civil Parish and Parish Ward of Inverurie; Burgh
Ecclesiastical Parish or Quoad Sacra Parish of Inverurie
School Board District of Inverurie

Shown here (see left and below) are the left and right-hand pages of the 1911 Census for Scotland. The details for line 1, for instance, are read right across the page and all relate to that individual person

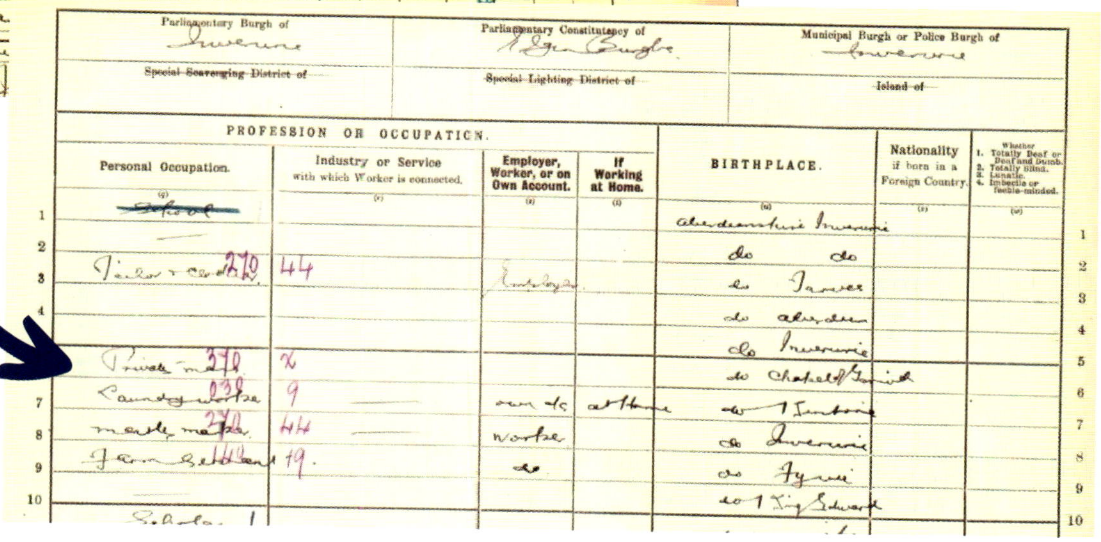

Parliamentary Burgh of Inverurie
Parliamentary Constituency of Elgin Burghs
Municipal Burgh or Police Burgh of Inverurie

PROFESSION OR OCCUPATION. Personal Occupation.	Industry or Service with which Worker is connected.	Employer, Worker, or On Own Account.	If Working at Home.	BIRTHPLACE.	Nationality if born in a Foreign Country.	Whether 1. Totally Deaf or Deaf and Dumb. 2. Totally Blind. 3. Lunatic. 4. Imbecile or feeble-minded.

Be sure not to miss the details for your ancestors on this right-hand page, inlcuding, as they do, valuable information about their occupations, birthplaces and more

The 1911 Census (Scotland)

For England, Wales and Ireland the 1911 Census records that we can see are the householders' schedules. This means that they are scans of the very forms that our ancestors filled in.

For the 1911 Census for Scotland the records we see are the Enumerators' Summary Books. This means that, like the 1841 to 1901 Census returns of England, Wales and Scotland, they are summaries which have been collated by the census enumerator (the person tasked with distributing the forms and collecting them in from the households).

While it's a shame that we can't see the householder schedules for the 1911 Census for Scotland it does, similarly to the census records of the other countries, contain the increased collection of details that we can enjoy studying for 1911.

3 useful census search tips

- Go to your chosen census website and enter in the details you know about your ancestor (eg name, birth year, place they lived).

- When searching it's tempting to enter as precise details as possible. If you are not successful doing this, then you need to cast your net wider, and search on ranges of dates and variations in spellings. For instance, just a small error (such as a different age, or a spelling mistake, might mean that you don't find the entry for your ancestor). Many of our ancestors may have had low (or no) levels of literacy meaning that such errors and variations in spellings are all too possible.

- As is the case with all family history research, you need to work backwards in time – for instance finding your ancestor on the 1911 Census, then the 1901, then the 1891 etc. If you don't search methodically backwards, then you might end up searching someone with the correct name, but who isn't actually someone on your family tree!

Where to search the census online

For Scotland your go-to site will be **www.scotlandspeople.gov.uk** – here you will be able to search indexes and view images of the census records, 1841-1921. You can also find indexes and transcriptions to the 1841-1901 Censuses for Scotland widely available. For instance try **www.freecen.org.uk** and if you are a member of one of the main genealogy websites see if they have indexes and transcriptions of the Scottish census records too.

For England and Wales, sites such as Ancestry, Findmypast, MyHeritage and TheGenealogist, allow you to view images. FreeCen has transcriptions, and so does FamilySearch.org (for FamilySearch, you will need a subscription to Findmypast.co.uk to view images or visit one of the FamilySearch family history centres located worldwide).

For Ireland your go-to census site is **www.census.nationalarchives.ie**

Start with the most recently available census and work backwards, following your families every 10 years until 1841. Use census returns to corroborate facts in BMD records (and vice-versa) but keep an open mind; our ancestors may not have known where they were born or when, and were not always completely honest about their age, marital status or, for example, whether the youngest child recorded was their own or an illegitimate grandchild.

USEFUL CENSUS WEBSITES

FREE INDEX WEBSITES

You can find free indexes to the census at:

- at https://freecen2.freecen.org.uk/ (1841-1891)
- and http://familysearch.org (1841-1911 England & Wales; 1841-1891 Scotland)

SUBSCRIPTION SITES WITH ORIGINAL DOCUMENT IMAGES

To search indexes and view copies of the original census pages for England and Wales 1841-1911 go to the digitised collections of the census available at the following subscription sites. The 1921 Census for England and Wales is currently only available at Findmypast.co.uk:

- www.ancestry.co.uk
- www findmypast.co.uk
- www.thegenealogist.co.uk
- www.myheritage.com
- www.familyrelatives.com (1841-1901 Censuses available)

To see the census records for Scotland 1841-1921 (accessed via paid credits) see www.scotlandspeople.gov.uk
And to see census records for Ireland 1901-1911 complete records (free access to the images) see www.census.nationalarchives.ie (plus fragments from the 1821-1851 Census records)

Tip

Many public libraries offer free access to Ancestry and Findmypast. Enquire at your local library to see if they do. Alternatively free trials are often available at the main subscription websites.

Making the most of DNA

Day by day the potential of DNA to help you with your family tree research is growing exponentially. Get to grips with the basics, master the jargon, and find out how it can help you to make new discoveries in your family history

Which DNA test is best for me?

A It depends on whether you'd like to test specifically your fatherline (this requires a Y-DNA test), motherline (an mt-DNA test) or across all the branches of your genetic inheritance, – including your father- and motherline (autosomal tests).

Various Y-DNA tests are available, providing increasing detail about your Y-chromosome inheritance, the more you pay. Both Y-DNA and mt-DNA will tell you about your deep ancestry of your father- or motherline respectively – assigning you to a haplogroup, following which you can trace these lines back millennia. Only males have a Y-chromosome – so Y-DNA tests may only be taken by men. Both men and women inherit mt-DNA, so both may take such a test.

Autosomal tests are those that have captured the imagination of many millions of people and led to DNA testing becoming a mainstream pursuit. In addition to providing a broad brush picture of your ancestral ethnicity they can also be used in combination with traditional family history research to grow and verify your family tree, find new cousins, solve family mysteries and more.

I've not taken a DNA test, am I missing out?

A DNA will reveal information about the genetic material that you've inherited. You share 50% of your DNA with each of your parents. With each generation that you go back in time, you receive a smaller proportion, and – at some point – you will find that you don't share any DNA with your distant ancestors that is measurable by an autosomal test.

Your autosomal DNA test results will give you general clues to your ethnic heritage and will also provide you with DNA matches, giving a list of people with whom you share segments of DNA. The major family history DNA tests, Ancestry, FamilyTreeDNA, MyHeritageDNA, 23andMe, also provide useful tools to help you work out who and how you're related to others.

Only you can decide if you're missing out by not doing a DNA test. By not testing you do avoid the ethical dilemmas that you might face if you do test (for example, revelations of family secrets), however you will also miss out on the opportunities to find further relations and solve research brickwalls. Bear in mind that DNA isn't an alternative to traditional genealogical research; rather it's an additional tool to use to learn more about your family history.

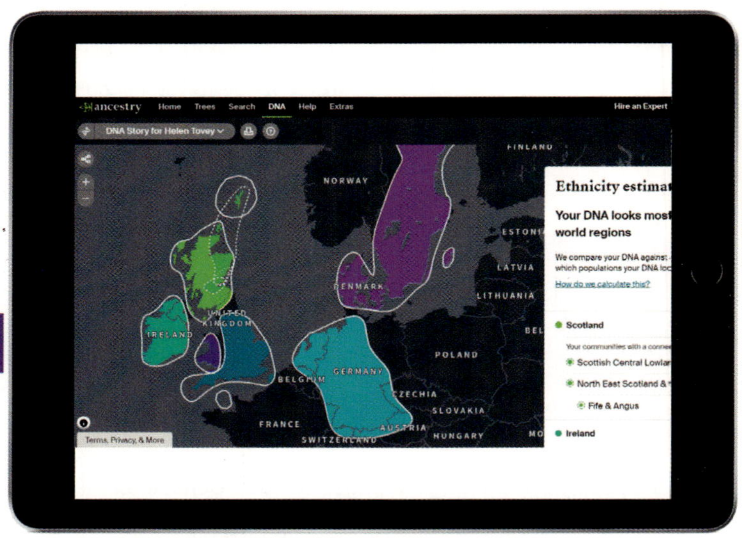

'Ethnicity estimates' have an immediate appeal, piquing the interest of family history enthusiasts (and others), but they are just the tip of the iceberg regarding the discoveries and tools you can make when using DNA in your research

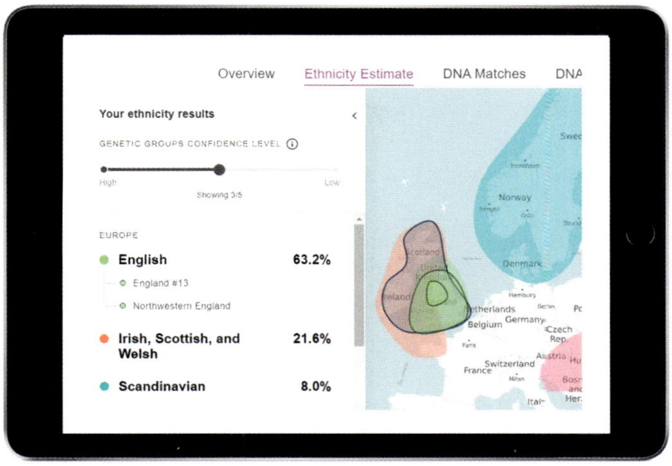

How much does a DNA test cost?

A Below are the usual retail prices at the time of going to print. It's well worth keeping an eye out for discounts and special offers, which are often run over holiday seasons on DNA kits. Please note also that the prices below do not include shipping costs.

- Ancestry autosomal £79
- LivingDNA autosomal £99
- MyHeritageDNA autosomal £79
- 23andME autosomal £79
- FamilyTreeDNA autosomal US$79 (Family Finder); Y-DNA from FamilyTreeDNA from US$119; mt-DNA from FamilyTreeDNA US$159

My cousin has tested with a different company to me, how can I compare our results?

A It's possible to download and upload DNA test results between a number of DNA test companies – meaning that you can ensure you've got your DNA test results in multiple DNA test site databases. Not all test companies allow this but you and your cousin will be able to find compatibility – ie get your results on the same site somehow, and then compare your results. To get your DNA into the Ancestry or 23andMe databases then you need to test with either of those companies directly as they do not allow uploads of tests from other sites.

How does DNA help with traditional family tree papertrail research?

A DNA can shed light on entirely new people and lines to investigate and may also be used to prove or disprove existing lines of research. For instance, it can make you aware of a connection to a distant relation's online family tree – one that you might never have become aware of otherwise. Alternatively, it can help to break down brickwalls, eg by resolving research roadblocks between two people of the same name.

As well as a map, the ethnicity reports will also give you a percentage breakdown, as shown in this example for MyHeritage, see left. If you have your DNA test results in more than one company's database you will be able to compare how each report on your ethnicity estimate: there are very likely to be both similiarities and differences

New lines to investigate

The first step on getting your DNA test results back will probably be a curious look through your ethnicity report. Next you'll turn to your list of DNA matches – and it's here that you'll see how your traditional research and your DNA discoveries are going to go hand in hand. Your DNA will give you new leads to explore, to find living relatives today, and note the possible way in which you are both related; your traditional research (and theirs) will equip you with the details (names, dates, places) you need to determine exactly how you are related.

Most of the matches in your list will be distant relations, eg fourth cousins or further. This means that you and they share a 2x or 3x great-grandparent. You have 16 great-great-grandparents and 32 great-great-greats. So you can see that a thorough piecing together of your family history – using the traditional clues of names, dates and places – is vital on the quest to work out exactly how you and your match are related and where you each fit on each other's tree. Note – you both need to have undertaken traditional research to be able to corroborate those names etc. If one of you has done more research than the other, you may be able to help ▶

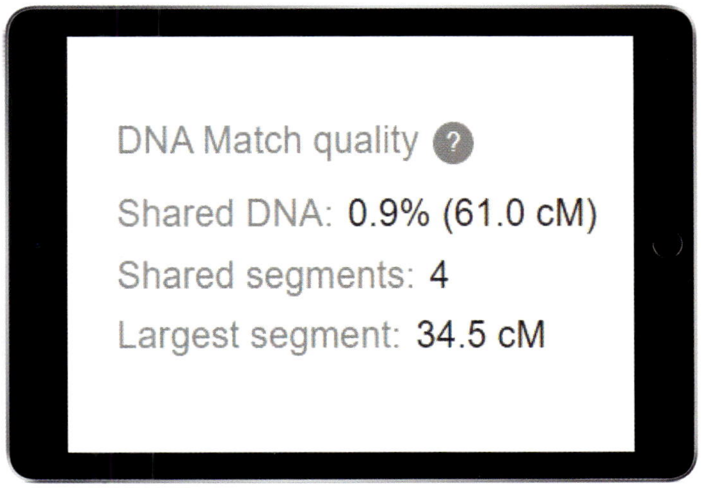

In your DNA matches list on MyHeritage you'll see the percentage of DNA you share with a match, the number of centiMorgans shared, the number of segments shared, and the size of the largest segment shared

[Continues on page 93]

Glossary

DNA has a language of its own, one you may be unfamiliar with, but it's worth getting to grips with it to help you make use of genetics in your genealogy. We have included only those words that crop up really frequently when talking about DNA and family history. Some are general scientific terms and others are phrases that have evolved, specific to the genealogy community.

autosome (atDNA or auDNA) – an autosome is a chromosome, other than the sex chromsomes. Humans typically have 22 pairs of autosomes and one pair of sex chromosomes (allosomes).

admixture – the more correct term for 'ethnicity report', each of our admixture refers to our geographic origins as interpreted by our DNA.

alleles – a specific form of a gene. Our genes have the capacity for a number of different outcomes. The allele is that outcome. Eg the gene may code to give us a trait, such as brown eyes.

base pair (bp) – a rung on the DNA ladder, each base pair is made up of a pair of chemicals. The chemicals are adenine (A), which pairs with thymine (T), and guanine (G), which pairs with cytosine (C). The information about your base pairs is included in your raw DNA data.

centiMorgan – a unit for measuring genetic linkage. From a genealogy point of view the importance lies in number of centiMorgans you share with a match – more centiMorgans tends to mean a closer relationship (the number of shared centiMorgans can vary within ballpark parameters).

chromosomes – these are found inside the nucleus of a cell. Inside each chromosome is DNA. Humans typically have 23 pairs of chromosomes.

chromosome browser – a tool displaying which segments of chromosome you and a DNA match share. 23andMe, FamilyTree DNA, MyHeritage and DNAPainter all provide chromosome browser tools.

FIR fully identical region – identical segments of chromosomes between you and a match. The DNA of siblings typically comprise 25% FIRs; identical twins have 100% FIRs.

genes – these are made of DNA. Humans each have about 24,000 genes.

haplogroup – the group to which you are assigned, based on your match to a common ancestor on your maternal and/or paternal lines. (Males can be assigned to two haplogroups – mother's side and father's side; females can just be allocated to a haplogroup on their mother's side). Each haplogroup is given a name consisting of a letter and number combination.

IBD identical by descent – an identical segment between two or more matches of DNA inherited from a common ancestor.

IBS identical by state – identical segments aren't shared with a common ancestor, so are just a false positive. IBP (identical by population) is an identical segment of DNA that is shared by many people in a population group (ie also not useful for precise family history purposes).

MPE misattributed-paternity event – a DNA result that reveals an unexpected proportion of DNA between a child and its parent. Eg a child gets 50% of DNA from each biological parent (and shares about 3,400 centiMorgans with each parent). A misattributed-paternity event several generations ago will still be reflected in the DNA inheritance of the offspring with half relationships.

phylogenetic tree – a diagram showing branches of descent from a common ancestor. Haplogroups and their evolution can be mapped as a phylogenetic tree.

segment – a shared segment is a stretch of identical chromosome shared between you and a match. The longer the unbroken segment the more closely you tend to be related to your match.

SNP (single nucleotide polymorphism) – SNPs are pronounced 'snips'. A SNP is a variation in a single nucleotide. When our genes recombine changing occurs in the coding. This variation is called a SNP. As mentioned above, a shared segment is a stretch of identical chromosome. Each end of the segment is determined by a SNP, and the distance between the two SNPs is referred to in centiMorgans.

subclade – a subgroup of a haplogroup.

DNA to-dos

Taking a DNA test is just the first step. To get the most from your results there is much to be learned and many projects and tasks to do. They take time and care but will reward you with further insights and discoveries to your family history. Here are 3 things you can do with your DNA test results.

Explore the automated theoretical trees
Many of the DNA testing companies offer tools to help you. For example, Ancestry ThruLines and MyHeritage Theory of Relativity both compare your DNA with others on your match list and draw in traditional family tree material on their websites to help determine how your family trees fit together. The more traditional research you've undertaken yourself, the more readily you'll be able to verify (or dismiss) these potential ancestors.

Upload & download your raw DNA
To maximise your chances of making matches, it's worth downloading your raw DNA and uploading it to other DNA companies' websites too (where possible).

- For a chart showing which companies accept uploads, see **https://familytr.ee/updowndna**
- For instructions on how to download and upload your raw DNA see **https://familytr.ee/updowninstructions**

DNA projects

Y-DNA – like surnames – is inherited father to son. Check out the listing of 11,476 DNA projects on https://www.familytreedna.com/group-project-search – perhaps your name is listed? If not is it time to start your own surname DNA project?

Register your interest for a DNA course
Family Tree runs online courses in DNA for absolute beginners and people at more advanced stages too. To register your interest and be notified of upcoming courses, prices, dates, etc, please email enquiries@family-tree.co.uk with 'DNA learning' in the subject line.

Take a free trial to FamilyTreePlus & come along to the DNA Club
FamilyTreePlus is an online membership for family history enthusiasts from the publishers of *Family Tree*; with FamilyTreePlus members gain access to a minimum of three live club meetings per month (one of which is the DNA Club), plus they can read the library of *Family Tree* back issues & get the latest issue of *Family Tree*. To find out how to get your free trial, visit **www.family-tree.co.uk/membership**

[Continued from page 91]

each other.

Thus, in some respects – it's not how DNA can help your traditional research, but how traditional research can transform your understanding of your DNA match list. However, without that match list you'd have had to be researching far and wide to find that distant cousin, with whom you can now strike up a genealogy friendship, and perhaps share family anecdotes, clues and of course photographs too.

Break down research roadblocks

Where DNA unquestionably comes into its own is in opening new avenues of research, and in overcoming roadblocks. If you are stuck on an identified ancestor (eg an unnamed father), your DNA results list can show a match, whose direct and indirect branches may be researched to reveal likely candidates. Conversely you may have a name to work with but may have few other clues. Or perhaps you have two (or more) possibilities sharing the same name, but are unsure which of the possible leads is yours. If so, DNA may help to determine the correct person to follow up.

Just as with traditional research, the more details you know the better, so it is with DNA. For instance, by the time you get to your second cousins you may only share about 3% of your DNA, and for third cousins it's not even 1%. However, by encouraging your wider family to test you can compare and pool that information, so increasing your success rate in making sense of your matches.

HOW TO SEARCH, SORT & FILTER YOUR DNA MATCHES WITH ANCESTRYDNA

It's astonishing how many DNA matches you can get isn't it – but how can you start to make sense of them all? The DNA testing companies each provide tools to help you do just this. Here we're going to look at some of the tools provided by AncestryDNA, to help you search, sort and filter your DNA matches.

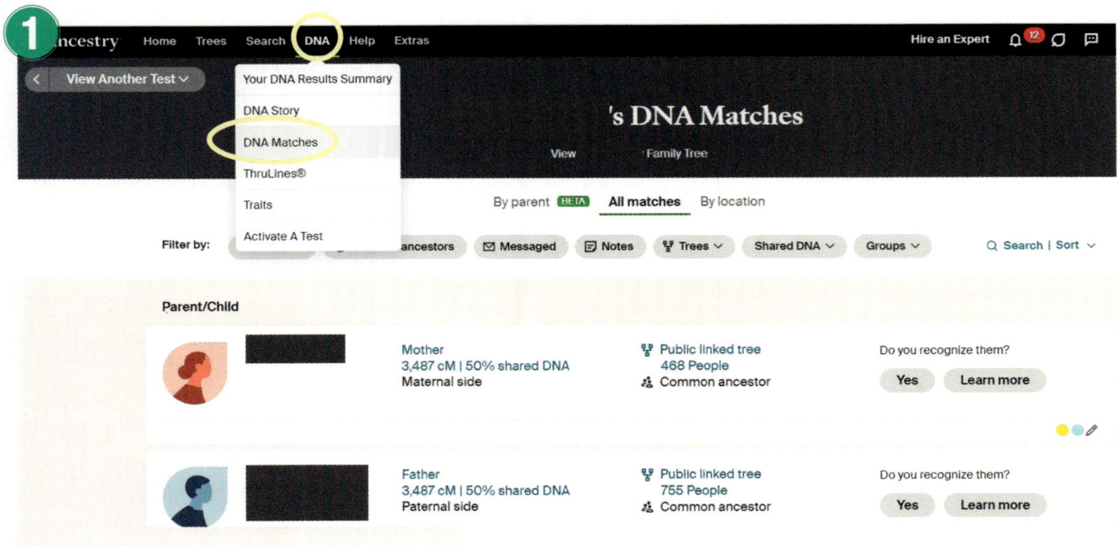

First go to Ancestry. From the menu choose 'DNA', then 'DNA Matches'. Here you will see many of the tools that will help you work on your DNA matches on Ancestry.

TIP! Spend time exploring each of the options, experimenting on your DNA match list. Don't worry – you can't 'break it'!

HOW TO SEARCH YOUR DNA MATCHES

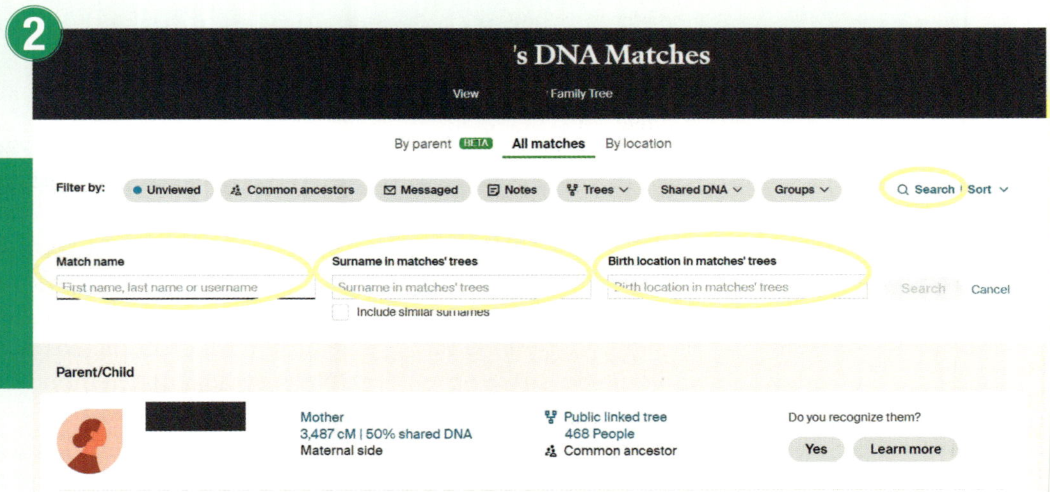

Selecting 'Search' reveals three fields, allowing you to search by match name, surnames and birth locations in your matches trees. Usefully you can search on more than one field at a time: this means that instead of just searching on the surname 'Linton' you can search on people in your matches' trees who had the surname Linton and were also born in, for instance, 'Hawick, Roxburghshire, Scotland' etc – making your search results much more specific.

HOW TO SORT YOUR DNA MATCHES

There are two sort options: either to sort your DNA match list by 'Relationship: close to distant', or by 'Date: newest to oldest'.

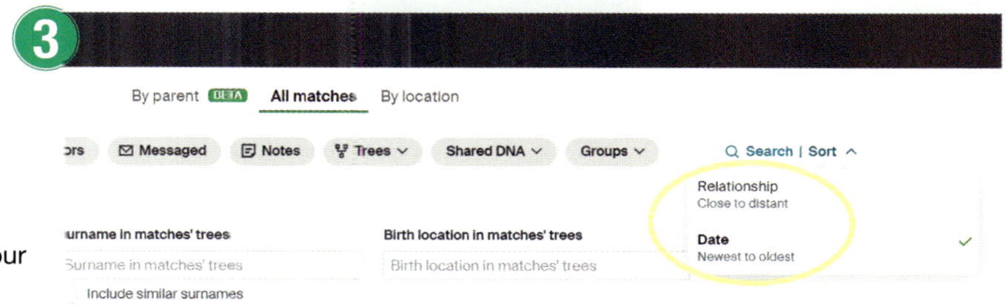

HOW TO FILTER YOUR DNA MATCHES

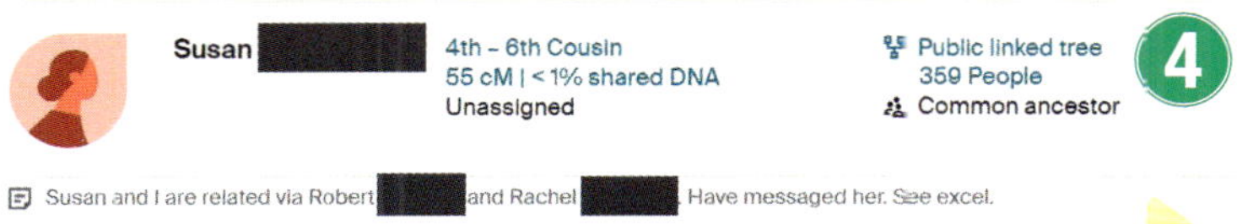

There are extensive filtering options on Ancestry. 'Unviewed', 'Messaged' and 'Notes' are self-explanatory.

NOTES: It is well worth making sure you use the 'Notes' field to record your thoughts and deductions. Clicking on 'Notes' will bring up a list of everyone for whom you've written a note. In addition, when scrolling through your DNA match list you'll be able to see the note you've made about a DNA match displayed below their name too.

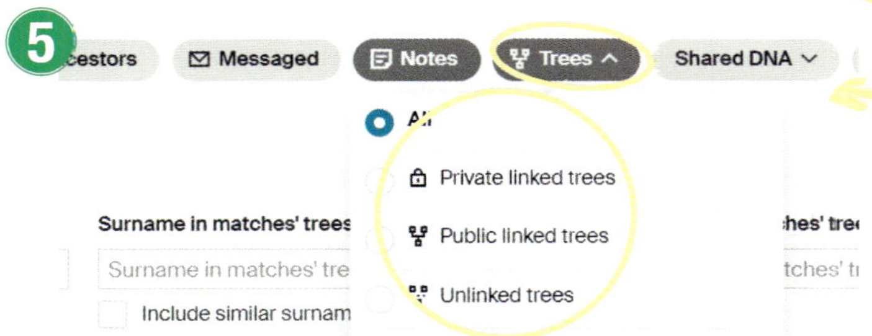

TREES: Using the 'Trees' filter you can opt top to view only those matches with 'Private linked trees', 'Public linked trees' or 'Unlinked trees'.

Linked tree?! If you've not done so already it can be a good idea to link your tree to your DNA kit. This will mean that the Ancestry algorithm can provide you with 'common ancestor' hints (see below).

HOW TO LINK YOUR TREE

To find out how to link your tree, follow the advice here: **https://support.ancestry.co.uk/s/article/Linking-an-AncestryDNA-Test-to-a-Tree**

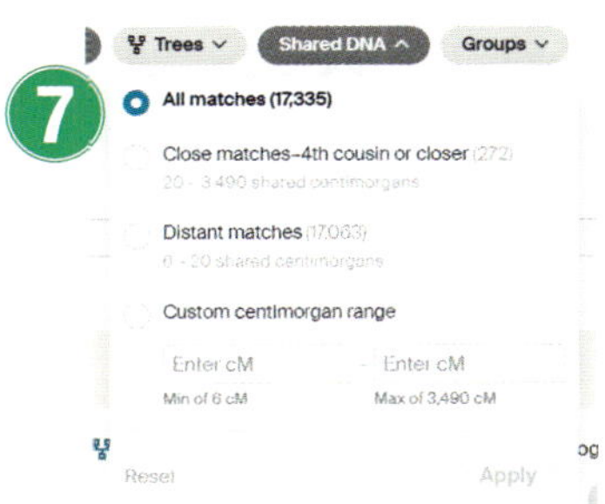

SHARED DNA: With the 'Shared DNA' filter you can home in on sub-sets of your DNA match list, to view close matches, distant matches, or only those matches that fall within a customised centimorgan range that you determine.

COMMON ANCESTORS: This provides you with a list of DNA matches that have an ancestor in their tree that you also have in your tree. To see how it works, select one of your DNA matches to view their tree and the common ancestors will be outlined in green.

LEARN MORE ABOUT DNA

Learn more about DNA with the DNA Workbook available from **www.family-tree.co.uk/store/genealogy-tools/family-tree-magazine/dna-workbook/** priced £20 plus p&p

GROUPS: Ancestry provide you with the option to sort your DNA matches into groups. You can create customised groups, each with its own colour-coded dot and a name of your choosing. The groups are entirely created by you. You can continue to add and remove people as you wish, can edit the name, or even delete your group or groups as you wish.

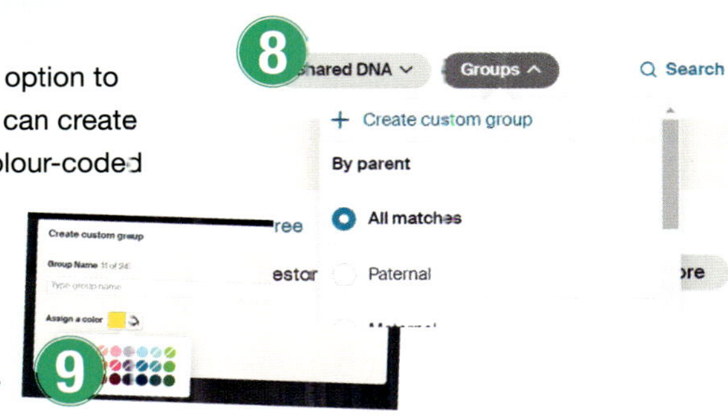

HOW TO GROUP YOUR DNA MATCHES

To find out how to put your DNA matches into groups, follow the advice here: **https://support.ancestry.co.uk/s/article/Grouping-and-Filtering-AncestryDNA-Matches**

OTHER DNA TOOLS

Taking a DNA test really is just the first step. Here is a selection of other DNA tools you may find useful to explore to learn more about your DNA.

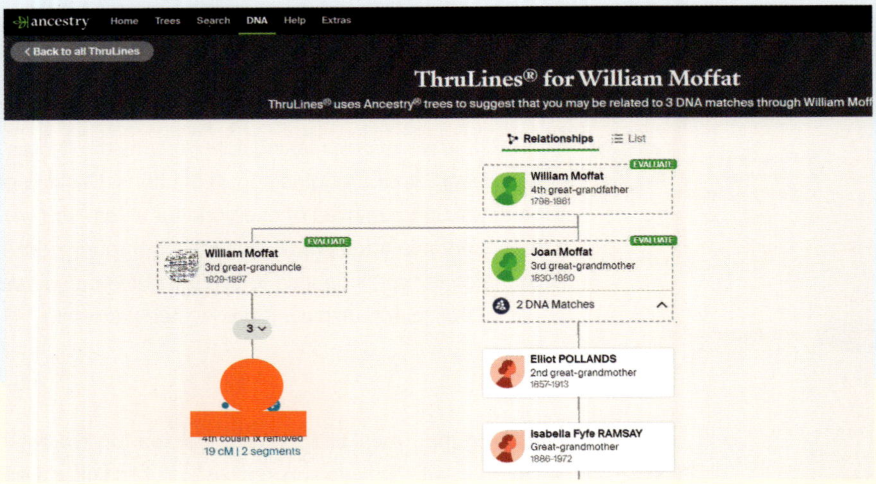

Ancestry ThruLines: These are generated when common ancestors are found in your online Ancestry tree and in the tree(s) of one or more of your DNA matches. The ancestors that you have in your tree are coloured pink or blue. People coloured green as those that you do not yet have in your family tree. This is why they are labelled 'evaluate': you need to work out whether it is accurate to include them in your family tree. You do so, by doing traditional family history research, i.e. looking at the records (census, parish registers, birth certificates etc).

Ethnicity estimates: To the right is the ethnicity estimate provided for a DNA test taker by Ancestry, and below that is the one provided by MyHeritage for the same DNA test taker. As you will see they are significantly different from each other. The ethnicity estimates are some of the most immediately popular aspects of DNA testing but they are 'estimates' – and they will change over time. They are fun to look at, but not the most useful aspect of DNA testing when it comes to doing family history research. It's your DNA matches that will help you make discoveries about your ancestors.

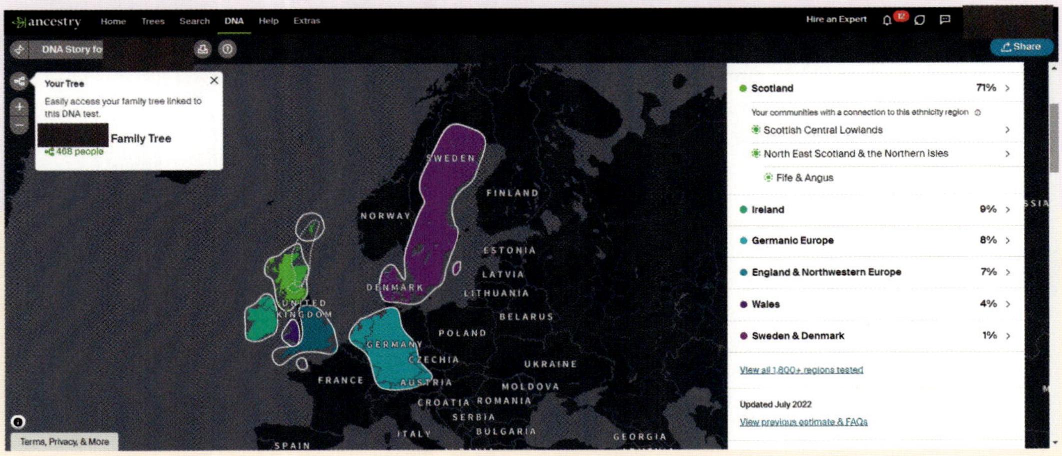

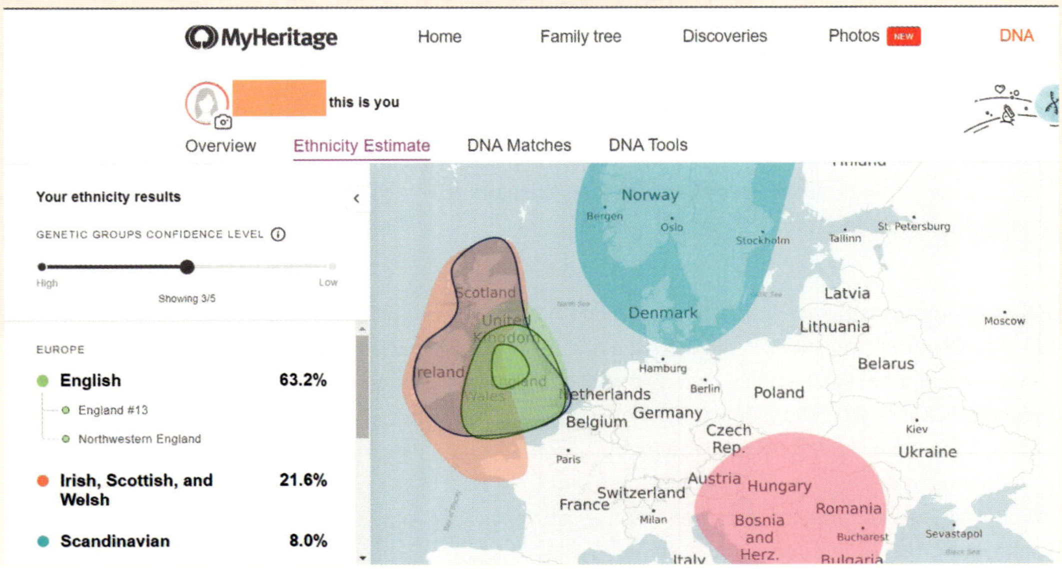

Chromosome browser: MyHeritage provides a Chromosome Browser. Using it you can compare the segments of DNA that up to 7 of your DNA matches, match with you. Only the first five chromosomes are displayed here – but 22 chromosomes are included in the browser. The XX or XY pair of chromosomes is not included. Remember that your chromosomes come in pairs.

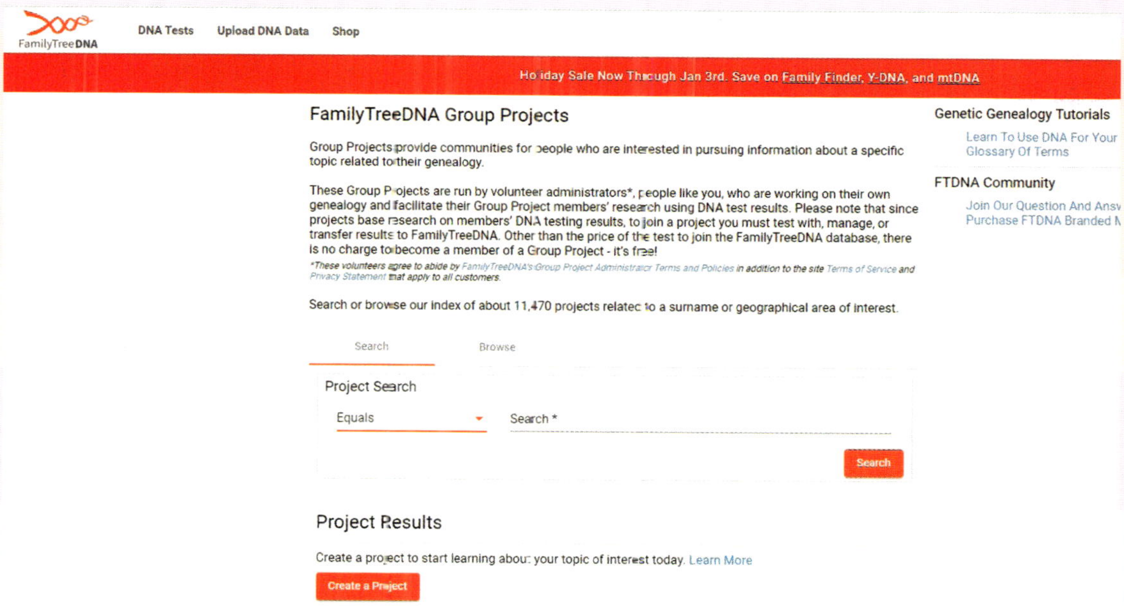

Y-DNA & mtDNA: If you're looking for a Y-DNA test (to learn about your father's father's line) or an mtDNA test (to learn about your mother's mother's line) then the website you need is www.familytreedna.com. As surnames in many cultures around the world are passed down the father's line, then Y-DNA testing and surname projects go hand-in-hand. FamilyTreeDNA provides the tools needed to set up a DNA project and collaborate with other researchers. To date there are more than 11,470 DNA projects – linked to a surname or a geographical area. Find out more about them at www.familytreedna.com/group-project-search

HOW HAVE YOU GOT ON?

We hope you've enjoyed exploring the websites covered in the *Family History Workbook for Beginners*, have begun creating your family tree, and had a successful foray into the family history records that can be found online. We also hope you've found the check lists, family tree charts and resources available from **www.family-tree.co.uk/information/fhwfb** useful for keeping your family history organised.

Starting your family history is just the first step. Many people find that it becomes a part of their lives, something to dip in and out of, something to absorb them everyday perhaps. It's entirely up to you how you do your family history, where you focus your energy – each and every one of our family stories is unique, and it's so great that you are taking the time to research and record yours.

To help you continue on your genealogy journey, the family history community is there to help you. From joining a family history society or Facebook group, to attending a webinar, signing on for a course, and reading family history books and magazines, there are many avenues open to you, to help you learn more and more about how to do family history.

WHAT'S NEXT?

The Family History Workbook for Beginners is published by the publishers of *Family Tree*, the UK's longest-running family history magazine, and hosts of Family Tree Plus, the online community for family historians that provides online meetings on research know-how, DNA and family history kit every month. See page 99 to find out more...

WHAT'S NEXT FOR YOU?

We have some great ideas to help you learn more about family history!

❶ Join the club – become a member of Family Tree Plus and attend the monthly, live, online meetings of the Study Club, DNA Club and Genealogy Gadgets Club. Plus get the latest issue of *Family Tree* as a digital read, AND a searchable library of *Family Tree* too. Prices start from £9.99 per month. See **www.family-tree.co.uk/store/membership-subscriptions**

❷ Read up on family history – subscribe to *Family Tree* magazine and receive the latest issue every month. *Family Tree* is available as a print or digital issue. Prices start from £5 for the first three issues; £12.99 per quarter thereafter. See page 87 of the *Workbook* for details.

❸ Get the latest – sign up for the free enewsletter and receive regular family history updates, advice, offers and more. See page 55 of the *Workbook* and sign up at **www.family-tree.co.uk/account/register**

Inspired by The National Archives' records discovered on Ancestry
It started with his name.
Which led me to a secret wedding at Gretna Green. She signed with a signature and he with a cross.
Illiterate, with a baby imminent, he took his hand to the loom. But the changing times must have forced that hand into finding other work. Again and again.
Our cities were transformed by people willing to turn their hand to anything. I discovered he was one of them. My Great Grandad. Arthur Wade.
Bring your backstory to life with a 14-day free trial.*
ancestry
*One free trial per person. Requires registration with valid credit or debit card. Unless you cancel before the end of your free trial, your chosen membership will begin and you'll be charged the relevant price Membership will automatically renew at same price at end of each membership period, unless you are notified otherwise. Cancel at least two days before renewal date by visiting your MyAccount section or by calling 0800 404 9723 if you do not wish to renew.